WORLD BANK WORKING PAPER NO. 190

Governance of Technical Education in India

Key Issues, Principles, and Case Studies

Edited by Andreas Blom and Jannette Cheong

THE WORLD BANK
Washington, D.C.

ISBN: 978-0-8213-8341-4
eISBN: 978-0-8213-8355-1
ISSN: 1726-5878   DOI: 10.1596/978-0-8213-8341-4

Library of Congress Cataloging-in-Publication Data has been requested.

Contents

Tables

Figures

Foreword

Tertiary education, particularly technical and engineering education, is critical to realize the Indian dream of becoming a competitive player in the global knowledge economy. As part of the endeavor to improve quality of educational institutions in the tertiary sector, the aim has been to enhance their autonomy. Autonomy and accountability go hand in hand. The situation calls for continuous learning on the part of institutions—how to respond to the rapidly changing environment without compromising quality. I am extremely happy to know that the *Learning Forum* convened under the aegis of the Technical Education Quality Improvement Program (TEQIP), including this publication, has deliberated these issues in great length and depth. I am sure that the outcomes shall be extremely useful to fine-tuning our technical education programmes.

Kapil Sibal
Minister of Human Resource Development
Government of India

Acknowledgments

The state government delegations and institutional leaders, who took interest and invested considerable amount of their time in the *Forum*, deserve the highest recognition for their contribution to the event and this report. In particular, we acknowledge the contributions of State Secretaries, Commissioners, and Director of Technical Education: S. Sahariya, M. Biswas, A.S. Srikanth, L. P. Reddy, M. P. Gupta, S. K. Mahajan, S. Dasgupta, and H. U. Talawar. Indeed, the energy and commitment from the delegations showed just how important governance of technical education is in India: "*Good Governance is not an option.*"

The approval and encouragement of the Ministry of Human Resources Development was essential for this *Forum*. We thank the Honorable Minister Kapil Sibal for his foreword to this report. The support and facilitation by A. Thakur and R. Chowdhary was as always exemplary. The ever-helpful, patient, and pro-activeness of Prof. A.U. Digraskar and his team in the National Project Implementation Unit was equally greatly appreciated.

A key partner for the *Learning Forum* was the National Association of Software and Services Companies (NASSCOM). Rajdeep Sahrawat, Sandhya Chintala, Bidhan Kankate, Shruti Verma, Arjun Menon, and Avneet Bajaj from NASSCOM helped in the design and development of the program and supported the local organization of the *Forum*. NASSCOM's commitment to Indian education is remarkable and an example to industry associations globally.

The calls to arms from the *Forum*'s key speakers from industry and government were insightful and generated heated discussions. These speakers included, notably, S.P.K. Naidu I.A.S, Special Chief Secretary and Professor D. N. Reddy, Vice Chancellor, Jawaharlal Nehru Technological University, from Andhra Pradesh; and Vijay Thadani, CEO, National Institute of Information Technologies and Chairman of the Confederation of Indian Industry Education Committee.

The *Learning Forum* and this report would not have been feasible without the tremendous effort of Jannette Cheong, who led the planning and execution of the *Forum* and the report. Praise is also due to the high-level team of governance experts of Arun Nigavekar, Andrew Cubie, Aims McGuinness, and Tom Kimura, who went beyond the call of duty to see through this *Learning Forum* successfully. The logistic and administrative execution was superbly handled by Anne Kroijer with the helping hand of Renu Gupta and Elfreda Vincent.

Lastly, we are grateful for the financial support received from the funders of the World Bank's Governance Trust Fund. In this regard, the unwavering and speedy support from Guenter Heidenhof in the World Bank's Delhi office was greatly appreciated. We also valued the seed funding received from British Council through Sally Goggin and Parul Gupta for the planning meeting in Warangal.

This paper is a joint publication with NASSCOM and NPIU (National Project and Implementation Unit of TEQIP).

Andreas Blom and Kurt Larsen
World Bank

NASSCOM®

National Project Implementation Unit
(A Government of India Unit for World Bank Assisted Project for Technical Education)

About the Contributors

Aims McGuinness is a senior associate of the National Center for Higher Education Management Systems (NCHEMS) in the United States. He is also an authority on state governance and coordination of higher education in the United States, and member of a number of international reviews through OECD and the World Bank. He also acts as a facilitator and consultant for board development for the Association of Governing Boards of Universities and Colleges (U.S.) and has served as former chair of the Board of Trustees of the State Colleges in Colorado.

Andreas Blom is a senior Education economist in the World Bank's department for Human Development in South Asia. He has acted as task team leader for two teams working with the governments of India and Pakistan to improve quality, access, and financing of their higher education and training systems. He has authored several global and regional studies on the financing of higher education, student loans, labor markets, quality of education, and science, technology, and innovation.

Andrew Cubie is the chair of the Scottish Credit and Qualification Framework, a director of the Leadership Foundation for Higher Education in the UK, and senior independent director for Her Majesty's Inspectorate for Education, Scotland, and contributor to the EU and U.S. governance seminar programs on higher education. He has also acted as former chair of Edinburgh Napier University and of the Committee of Chairs of UK Universities.

Arun Nigavekar is the Raja Ramanna fellow at the Department of Atomic Energy, a senior advisor at Science and Technology Park, University of Pune, and former chair of the Indian University Grants Commission, former vice-chancellor of the University of Pune, and founding director of the National Assessment and Accreditation Council. He previously supported the establishment of INQAAHE (the International Network of Quality Assurance Agencies in Higher Education) in the program's early years.

Jannette Cheong is a World Bank consultant, former head of International Collaboration and Development, and associate director for Quality Assessment, Higher Education Funding Council for England, and Her Majesty's inspector for Further and Higher Education. She has also acted as a facilitator and advisor to international initiatives and collaborations and worked in partnership with international and national organizations and other bodies.

Rong Wang is associate professor and head of the Department of Education, Economics, and Administration, in the Graduate School of Education at Peking University. Her research spans the role of education in labor markets, financing of basic education and higher education, educational policy towards poor and minority areas, community colleges, private education, and governance structure of schools and universities.

State Governments of Andhra Pradesh, Haryana, Karnataka, and West Bengal. The delegations from these four states prepared concise and very informative case studies. These states form the avant-garde of reform implementation in Technical Education in India. They are committed to delivering improved governance in the context of their policies and strategies for greater higher education autonomy and improved accountability.

Tsutomu Kimura has served as advisor to Japan's Ministry of Education, Culture, Sports, Science, and Technology and president of the National Institution for Academic Degrees and University Evaluation from 1998 to 2009., president of Tokyo Institute of Technology from 1993 to 1997, board Member of INQAAHE from 2003 to 2005., and vice chair for the Central Council for Education from 2001 to 2007. In addition, he has served as member of Science Council of Japan from 2000 to 2008, board member for International Geotechnical Society from 1992 to 1996, and OECD expert regarding quality assurance for cross-border higher education from 2003 to 2006.

Acronyms and Abbreviations

ADC	Academic Degrees Committee
AFRC	Admission and Fee Regulatory Committee
AICTE	All India Council for Technical Education
APSCHE	Andhra Pradesh State Council for Higher Education
BOG	Board of Governors
CII	The Confederation of Indian Industry
CUC	Committee of University Chairs
DST	Department of Science and Technology
FICCI	Federation of Indian Chambers of Commerce and Industry
HEIs	Higher Education Institutions
HOD	Heads of Department
IIM	Indian Institute of Management
IISER	Indian Institute of Scientific Education, and Research
IIT	Indian Institute of Technology
IRG	Internally Generated Revenue
JNTU	Jawaharlal Nehru Technological University
MEXT	Ministry of Education, Culture Sports, Science and Technology
MEST	Ministry of Education, Science and Technology
MHRD	Ministry of Human Resources Development
NAAC	National Assessment and Accreditation Council
NASSCOM	National Association of Software and Services Companies
NBA	National Board of Accreditation
NIAD-UE	National Institution for Academic Degrees and University Evaluation
NIIT	National Institute of Information Technologies
NPIU	National Project Implementation Unit
OBC	Other Backwards Castes
QA	Quality Assurance
RGUKT	Rajiv Gandhi University of Knowledge Technology
SC	Scheduled Castes
SCHEV	State Council of Higher Education for Virginia
ST	Scheduled Tribes
TEQIP	Technical Education Quality Improvement Program
UGC	University Grants Commission
VTU	Visvesvaraya Technological University

Currency equivalents and denominations as of February 1, 2010

Rupee 46.36= US$1.00
Rs. 1 lac = Rs. 100,000 = US$2,157
Rs. 1 crore = Rs. 10,000,000 = US$215,703

Executive Summary

The Need for Change

Tertiary education, and in particular technical and engineering education, is critical to India's aspirations of strengthening its reputation as a major competitive player in the global knowledge economy. The system is huge and complex, and there is a consensus that reforms are imperative. Issues of fair access and affordable participation in higher education are critical if India is to empower its people with educational opportunities that allow individual potential to be fulfilled, and allow more Indian graduates opportunities for employment and to compete in an international arena.

There are approximately 2,400 technical/engineering institutions across India's 30 states, of which less than 8 percent of public institutions are autonomous. The demand for tertiary education continues. There has been a phenomenal growth in the number of private colleges across India in the last 20 years. Private colleges now deliver 85 percent of all technical and engineering education. The significant changes in supply and demand make it increasingly important to ensure that tertiary education systems and institutions are effectively and efficiently governed and managed to meet the needs of industry and society.

In addition, major higher education reforms are ongoing. There are significant initiatives that stress, among other key priorities, the importance of increasing autonomy and accountability in the tertiary education sector. Countrywide policies have continued to identify this as key to the delivery of these national needs and to improving the quality of learning and teaching outputs and outcomes.[1] There is now an even greater commitment and imperative to implementing these reforms.

As key national changes are imminent, stakeholder groups represented at the *Learning Forum* emphasized the importance of working in partnership, so that overlapping interests can support a more effective delivery of education to meet the needs of society and industry. Good governance is an area where effective partnerships are crucial. Strengthening links with industry and local communities could also support a range of development opportunities for courses, faculty and most importantly the student experience and education and research outcomes.

These priorities are in line with the second phase of the Technical Education Quality Improvement Project and the need for ongoing capacity building. Developing effective governance will underpin long-term developments.

What Is Good Governance?

The *Learning Forum* reflected on the current global crisis and examples of failed and ineffective governance. This led to discussion of *why good governance is important*, and how fundamental principles are needed in an autonomous higher education system—as with all autonomous institutions that serve public interests.

Much has been written about good governance, both in higher education and in the corporate sector by international contributors. Clearly, in the corporate and banking sectors over recent years many bitter lessons have been learned. This includes examples like Enron in the United States and Satyam in India, where boards of governors failed in their essential duties. Higher education can gain from these experiences, but the different circumstances of learning institutions should not become limited in seeking to follow any current corporate model. In regard to good governance the public and not-for-profit sectors have much also to contribute:

- Good governance underpins and supports the mission and purpose of the institution. Without such shared intent in purpose and delivery a board of governors (BOG) will be weak.
- Good governance creates a sound, ethical and sustainable strategy, acceptable to the institution as a whole and other key stakeholders.
- Good governance oversees the implementation of such strategy through well-considered processes and procedures in an open, transparent and honest manner.
- Good governance is essential to the grant or assertion of autonomy. Boards of governors, by embracing good governance approaches, accept unequivocally their own collective and individual responsibilities.
- Good governance is not optional.

More on the basic *Principles and Challenges for Governance* discussed at the forum may be found in Chapter 2. The key principles and challenges for governance were further summarized at the *Forum* as follows:

For states:

- Establish deliverable policies for public benefit, which include a clear place for higher education
- Create autonomous structures for institutions
- Establish clear criteria for interventions
- Embed in finance policy support for higher education and institutional mission.

For institutions and their governing bodies: governing bodies should:

- Act as the custodian of values, mission and purpose
- Assert its autonomy and accountability
- Be unambiguously and collectively responsible for oversight
- Keep its effectiveness under objective review.

Learning Forum Objectives

The *Learning Forum* for Governance in Technical and Engineering Education was a joint initiative of the World Bank and the National Project Implementation Unit (NPIU) for the Technical Education Quality Improvement Program (TEQIP) of the Government of India.[2]

It was a pilot initiative that took place in Hyderabad from 23-26 September 2009 in partnership with state governments, the Ministry of Human Resource Development (MHRD) and the National Association of Software and Services Companies (NASSCOM),[3] following the completion of TEQIP-I, and before the start of TEQIP-II.

The key objectives for the *Learning Forum* were:

- To assist the participating state governments and institutions to obtain better education and learning outcomes through more strategic, purposeful and effective governance of their technical and engineering education institutions.
- To facilitate an exchange of learning and sharing of good governance policy and practice developments, barriers, and issues across the participating Indian states and internationally.
- To develop a conceptual framework for a learning forum on governance as a tool to further build capacity of senior policy makers and institutional leaders responsible for technical and engineering education. This tool should be evaluated through this pilot with the intention to facilitate other learning fora under the auspices of TEQIP-II. Additional fora would promote the sharing of knowledge, experience, and good practice to build capacity and assist sustainable development in other Indian states.

Inputs and Process

The *Learning Forum* brought together:

- Senior policy makers and institutional leaders from five states:[4] Andhra Pradesh, Haryana, Karnataka, Maharashtra, and West Bengal
- Ministry of Human Resource Development
- National experts from academia and industry
- Independent international consultants, World Bank, and NPIU staff.

(See participants list in Appendix A and more detail on the *Forum* inputs in Appendix B)

The *Learning Forum* required a significant amount of content preparation by the core forum team and participants. A half-day planning meeting was held in The National Institute of Technology, Warangal in January 2009 and a detailed planning and vision document was produced.

To provide an appropriate basis and comparative context for discussions, case studies were developed in advance of the *Learning Forum*: Generic papers on the principles, challenges, and common language of governance (Chapter 2); five state case studies (Chapter 3), and a national India and seven international case studies (Chapter 4), and twenty institutional case studies.

The principal steps of the process of the four-day *Forum* were as follows:

- First half of the *Forum* focused at state level, the second at the institutional level, finishing with conclusions related to both states and institutions
- A mix of focused plenary and small group work to facilitate debate and discussion
- Plenary sessions using short presentations, and panels who responded to focused questioning from participants
- Invited speakers: Mr. S.P.K. Naidu I.A.S, Special Chief Secretary, Andhra Pradesh, and Mr. Vijay Thadani, CEO, NIIT and Prof D N Reddy, Vice Chancellor, JNTU, Andhra Pradesh.

All *Learning Forum* materials and presentations have been posted on the *Forum* website along with best examples identified by the participants. More information about the inputs from participants, invited speakers, and the *Forum* process is available in Appendix B.[5]

Notes

[1] The concept of Autonomy was first talked in Kothari Commission report in early sixties and have been reemphasized in several subsequent report in last six decades. The Government of India's **11th Five-Year Plan**, the **CABE Committee on Autonomy of Higher Education Institutions**, established by the Ministry of Human Resources (MHRD) (2005), and more recently, in the **Knowledge Commission's Report** *Toward a Knowledge Society: Three Years of the Knowledge Commission*, October 2008, and in *June 2009*, **The Yash Pal Committee Report**: *Report of 'The Committee to Advise on Renovation and Rejuvenation of Higher Education'*, all call for major reforms for Higher Education in India including *Improving the Governance of Engineering Institutions*.

[2] Technical/Engineering Education Quality Improvement Project (TEQIP): (http://www.npiu. nic.in/project_tech4.htm). TEQIP is a Government of India project supported by the World Bank to improve quality of technical education. The first phase, TEQIP-I, started in March 2003 and ended March 2009 covering 127 institutions from 13 states; including 18 centrally funded institutions, 68 state government funded institutions, 22 private unaided institutions and 19 polytechnics. The second phase, TEQIP-II, is expected to start April 2010.

[3] The National Association for National Association of Software and Service Companies (NASSCOM): www.nasscom.in

[4] The five states were invited based on performance in TEQIP-I. At the time of the TEQIP assessment all five states had a majority of well performing institutions in the areas of autonomy, accreditation, implementation, and in the utilization of funds.

[5] http://go.worldbank.org/DJOT7BW8R0.

CHAPTER 1

Outcomes: The Nine Key Governance Issues

Knowledge, experience, and key issues related to developing good governance in technical and engineering education for the five participating states were vigorously and openly shared, debated, and discussed at the *Learning Forum*. The key outcome was a summary of nine key governance issues identified and debated during the *Forum* discussions. These are as follows:

1. Conceptualize legal foundation for a new model of an autonomous institution to serve a public purpose. The model should be the same for institutions funded in part by the government as well as those receiving no government subsidy. Transition all current government-funded, government-aided and private non-aided institutions to this model.

2. Common legal framework for governance, consistent with the new model of an autonomous institution, which provides:

- Clear statements of responsibilities and relationships for the BOG, including composition of boards of governors, selection/nomination of members, powers, functions, and an inculcation and assessment of accountability (using national guidelines)
- Professional qualifications, experience, responsibilities and appointment of the (a) Vice Chancellor/Director, and (b) the senior institutional officials, including terms and conditions of service (with minimum standards set by the state and implemented by higher education institutions [HEIs])
- Internal governing structure of the institution, including the principal academic and administrative bodies within the institution.

3. **Strategic planning at institutional and state levels to ensure:**

- Alignment with national and state priorities for India's global competitiveness in the knowledge economy:
- Size, shape, and relationship
- Access and equity
- Affordability (this will need support from central government)
- Quality

- Research competitiveness
- Inclusiveness (gender, ethnicity, and so forth)
- Responsiveness to the need of industry and India's future economy (see also credit transfer under issue 4 below).

4. Common quality assurance policies and standards (such as those internationally benchmarked using accepted parameters to meet the needs of industry) including:

- Common framework for qualifications, specifying the knowledge and skills required for employment to establish credible national standards
- Curriculum frameworks/subject benchmarks to guide curriculum development (state/central government to specify minimum credits)
- Student assessment, and continuous quality improvement within institutions
- Assessment and certification of skills and competencies obtained through industry-based training and experience for partial credit toward degrees
- Quality assurance and accountability based on outcomes (at various levels: institution, state, central government)
- Policies and mechanisms for student mobility (including credit transfer) within and between institutions and states, and outside India
- Framework for faculty appraisal/faculty development scheme including training, needs analysis and funding.

5. Policies and formal mechanisms for industry/academic collaboration, including, but not limited to:

- Industry investment in higher education (in kind, and funding); this may need national incentives/ support
- Experts from private industry serving as faculty and researchers at institutions and faculty serving in industry
- Industry providing training for students and awarding of credit for industry-based training.

6. Professional development for faculty, institutional leaders and boards of governors to increase their capacity to assume increased responsibilities in autonomous institutions (quality assurance, curriculum development, and so forth)

7. Optimum utilization of resources, including, but not limited to:

- Sharing of faculty and other resources (laboratories, libraries) among institutions
- Use of technology for effective delivery of courses and to support research.

8. Technical assistance and mentoring ("hand-holding") for institutions making the transition to autonomous status

9. Policy to tackle faculty shortage

It was clear from contributions made that the participating states have a sense of urgency and commitment to deliver the policies and practice pertinent to good governance for which they hold responsibility. However, it was also clear that the challenges faced are fundamental and complex.

Many key issues are multilayered and interlinked, involving institutions, state governments and central government—that is, national bodies. This can be seen in the list of nine key and 23 subcategories of governance issues listed above that were central to the discussion. States identified through discussion which bodies they considered would be responsible for taking responsibility and action.

There are number of areas in which states and institutions can take an effective lead in response to the nine key governance issues. These are separately summarized below for states, for institutions, and for the central government that is, national bodies. Further, a set of outcomes for TEQIP-II were identified for MHRD/NPIU and the World Bank.

Outcomes for States

Despite differences in the size and shape of technical and engineering education sectors (for example, in the percentage of provision through private non-aided colleges), it was agreed the participating five states face similar challenges and priorities for improvement. These can be summarized as:

- Developing a regulatory framework to ensure quality and public accountability in the face of extraordinary expansion of the sector, especially in private non-aided colleges
- Ensuring affordability and merit-based access
- Increasing institutional autonomy, in particular developing the capacity of boards of governors and institutional leaders to assume greater responsibility for delegated authority, and instituting new mechanisms for quality assurance and accountability
- Reforming standards and curricula to meet global expectations for graduates' knowledge and skills, and increasing relevance to regional, national and global labor market demands
- Strengthening links with industry/employers
- Strengthening the links between science and technology and regional economic development
- Addressing the severe shortage of qualified faculty and institutional leaders/managers.

The state case studies, chapter 3, and presentations at the *Learning Forum* provided examples of how the five states are leading in efforts to find solutions to these challenges. Among these reforms are:

- Reforms in regulations governing admission and establishment of common examinations for entrance into technical and engineering institutions
- Extending autonomy and other governance reforms by extending reforms initiated in TEQIP-I to all institutions, including establishment of boards of

governors, block grant funding patterns (at least for non-plan, non-salary components)

■ Strengthening the role of technical universities as a means to improve the quality of autonomous affiliated colleges

■ Strengthening the role of the state technical education departments' in promoting change and innovation, strengthening links with industry and regional economic development, promoting networking among institutions, and providing technical assistance and support for improvement at the university and college levels.

The *Learning Forum* reached consensus on nine key governance issues. With few exceptions, actions are required at every level of the system to address the issues: central authorities (MHRD, All India Council for Technical Education [AICTE], University Grants Commission [UGC], National Board of Accreditation [NBA], National Assessment and Accreditation Council [NAAC], or successor central regulatory authority), states, affiliating universities, and colleges. Nevertheless, the states can take the lead (either individually or through collective action) in several areas:

■ Review systematically the extent to which existing state laws, regulations, and overall capacity (for example, training and qualifications of state officials) support or serve as barriers to a transition from central state control to a new role of policy leadership and "steering at arm's length" for a network of autonomous institutions.

■ Review systematically existing state laws and regulations to ensure clear statements of responsibilities and relationships of boards of governors and professional qualifications of institutional leaders are consistent with a more decentralized accountable system.

■ Develop guidelines for effective performance of boards of governors and providing opportunities for boards of governors' members to participate in professional development events to keep abreast of latest developments in engineering/technical education and share best practices in board of governor leadership.

■ Sponsor state-level learning forums engaging the state's senior policy makers and industry/civic leaders to gain broader understanding and commitment to the changes in governance needed to support a globally competitive engineering/technical education system.

■ Undertake state-level strategic planning to ensure alignment of the technical/engineering education system with state and national priorities for competitiveness in the global knowledge economy. Engagement of key stakeholders, especially representatives of industry/employers, should be a key dimension of this planning.

■ Develop new mechanisms for establishing standards, curriculum, and quality assurance/accountability benchmarked to internationally accepted parameters. While central agencies must play a role in these initiatives, states (individually or in collaboration with each other) could lead in piloting new approaches that could serve as models to be implemented nationally. A key aspect of the state initiatives should be a further refinement of the role of technical universities in relationship to autonomous affiliated technical/engineering colleges.

■ Strengthen engagement of industry/employers at every level of the system, including ensuring that mechanisms are in place for consistent, sustainable, two-way communication and collaboration.

■ Provide professional development for state, university, and college officials to increase their knowledge and skills to assume new responsibilities in a more decentralized, flexible, transparent, and responsive system.

■ Provide technical assistance to institutions (boards of governors, vice chancellors/directors, and senior institutional leaders) to make the transition from state controlled to a more autonomous status.

Outcomes for Institutions

Despite differences in the size and shape of individual technical and engineering institutions and their legal and funding arrangements, there were clearly similar issues broadly identified for institutions in all five states.

■ There was a need to establish a clear statement of responsibilities and relationships for boards of governors, including composition of Boards, selection/nomination of members, their powers and functions and inculcation and assessment.

■ There was a need to ensure that institutions and stakeholders have both a clear and common understanding of what is meant by "autonomy" and "accountability."

■ There was a need to act in accordance with such accepted meanings.

■ There was a need to develop greater strength in the capacities of boards of governors.

■ Such additional strength would come in having regard to the professional qualifications, industry experience, and training of members of boards of governors.

Critically, all nine key governance issues, reached by consensus at the *Learning Forum*, reflect institutional needs. Again, with few exceptions, actions are required at every level of the system to address the issues. Involving institutions in effective partnership with state governments in particular, will be important and challenging, especially in states with a sizable tertiary sector.

Nevertheless, individual institutions can take a lead (either individually or through collective action involving institutions within one state or across states) in several areas:

■ Review the constituent documents of each institution to determine which support or serve as barriers to a transition from central state control to a new role of policy leadership for an autonomous institution. Prepare such amendments as may be necessary to facilitate change.

■ Develop guidelines for effective performance of boards of governors and provide opportunities for individual governors to participate in learning fora to keep abreast of latest developments in engineering/technical education and share best practice in governor leadership.

■ To respond to new standards, curricula and quality assurance policies and standards to be developed and benchmarked to internationally accepted parameters.

■ Strengthen effective engagement of industry/employers at every level of the institution, including ensuring that mechanisms are in place for consistent, sustainable, two-way communication and financially viable collaboration.

■ Participate in further learning fora at the institutional level, either individually or collectively, to enhance understanding of the changes in governance needed to support a globally competitive engineering/technical education system including the relationship of autonomous affiliated technical/engineering colleges to technical universities.

■ Provide sufficient funding and time for professional development for university, and college officials to increase their knowledge and skills to assume new responsibilities in a more decentralized, flexible, transparent, and responsive system.

Outcomes for the Consideration of the MHRD

A number of the key governance issues are national and require a coordinated response. The following are the key governance-related issues that involve the consideration of central government/national bodies:

■ All states and institutions desire more autonomy with accountability.

■ The conceptualization of a legal foundation for a new model of an autonomous institution to serve a public purpose—a model that could be applied to all institutions, both public and private.

■ The design of a legal framework for governance—consistent with the above model—that provides a clear statement of responsibilities and relationships for boards of governors (including the composition, recruitment, and selection, powers and functions, and assessment of accountability). The terminology used in implementation of such should be clearly and uniformly understood by all.

■ Policy statements reflecting national needs, for example, in relation to India's global competitiveness in the knowledge economy that provide a context for state governments and institutions' strategic planning in terms of size, shape, and relationships; access and equity; affordability; quality, research competitiveness; and inclusiveness (or in response to specific and immediate needs such as a faculty shortage crisis).

■ Common quality assurance policies and standards that are internationally benchmarked. For example, a qualifications framework with subject benchmarks to guide curriculum development, assessment, and certification of skills and competences. Information on quality and standards in accessible formats should be made available to students, parents, and other stakeholders.

- Governance of private institutions is important as 85 percent of technical and engineering institutions are in the private sector and need support and monitoring.
- Improved industry and academic collaboration to support industry investment in higher education and research, opportunities for training for industry, as well as industry's contribution to curricula, faculty and student development.
- Accessibility should be improved, maintaining quality; keeping in view the large population of the country.
- Need was expressed for credit transfers to enable movement of students from one institution to another and from state to state.
- Resource sharing, in terms of faculty and infrastructure facility should be encouraged within the state and outside including mobility of faculty.
- Policies for the utilization of new technology where these would bring efficiencies and development opportunities for states and institutions.

Outcomes for TEQIP for NPIU/MHRD and the World Bank

The *Forum* confirmed the centrality of strengthening governance policies and practice at the state and institutional level for quality of technical education. The MHRD/NPIU and the World Bank welcomed the opportunity to learn the following from the participating state governments and institutions:

- *Detailed and exciting information regarding states' growing experience of awarding autonomy to institutions and the ways that institutions have stepped up practices to empower, incentivize and hold accountable faculty.* Sharing these novel practices and policies across states and institutions would substantially improve the outcomes of technical education. This knowledge sharing is a task that MHRD/NPIU and the World Bank will continue to support through TEQIP-II.
- *Improved understanding of the balance between increased autonomy and strengthened accountability through effective boards of governors.* There is a clear need to improve the practices and capacities within institutional management, and in particular within boards of governors, to carry out effective strategies and oversight. Otherwise, increased autonomy and funding will not have its full returns, and could be abused. NPIU and the Bank should through TEQIP-II work in close partnership with states, affiliating universities, and institutions to assist the building of this capacity. That being said, the status quo in technical education may be overstated in terms of its achievements—when compared to practice elsewhere. Certain states and institutions are travelling at a snail's pace. TEQIP-II should encourage states and institutions to go "beyond their comfort zone" and reward reform implementation.
- *An acute awareness that TEQIP-II should provide strong performance information to state governments, boards of governors, and heads of institutions.* Sound state and institutional management requires credible benchmarking to position each institution in relation to others and assess performance. This information is presently not available in India, but will be put on fast track to pilot an

effective system for collecting and disseminating such performance information.

▪ *A need to enhance the guidelines for governance reforms in TEQIP-II* as described in the Project Implementation Plan, and a commitment to support governance priorities identified during the *Forum*.

▪ Finally, many other countries in the world currently are working on reforming the governance of their higher education system and institutions. Other countries, in particular in South Asia, can learn from the Indian experience of governance reforms. The *Forum*'s partnership and learning approach— bringing policymakers and institutional leaders together is one of such best practice Indian models that could inspire other countries in their governance reform efforts.

Next Steps

The dissemination of this report is the first next step. It is being circulated to the participating state governments and institutions. Further, it will be shared with states that did not participate to encourage them to take part in the autonomy and accountability reform of technical education.

The main follow-up will be through the agendas that state representatives and others have taken away from the *Learning Forum* either as action for cascading their learning, or as action plans that they may devise from the "Key Governance Issues" list and discussion. MHRD, NPIU, and the World Bank have set out their action in the paragraphs above and have adjusted the TEQIP-II implementation plan to assist states and institutions in their action plans.

Given the commonality of many issues there was considerable interest in Inter-state action in looking at solutions to the issues and barriers identified. The regular TEQIP-II review meetings could be one such opportunity for inter-state exchange of experiences.

Participating states are already taking the initiative to use the *Learning Forum* concept in their own states to disseminate experience and knowledge and also to encourage debate between key stakeholder groups regarding issues that affect them, and about which they may also re-examine their thinking and practices.

There was a clear, positive response to the *Learning Forum* initiative. In addition to the personal learning shared in the final session, senior leaders expressed a commitment to sharing not only the knowledge and experience they gained from their peers at the *Forum*, that is, for the benefit of their own states, but also a willingness to share their learning, ideas, knowledge and experience with other states in India. NPIU will organize future learning fora meetings as and when required based on the needs expressed by states/institutions subject to approval of MHRD as part of TEQIP-II.

CHAPTER 2

A Common Language and Key Principles of Governance

Andrew Cubie
Aims McGuinness

A Common Language for Governance?[1]

When considering aspects of governance both in the public, private and not-for-profit sectors it is easy to assume that in the use of a word or phrase there is an entire understanding. This is true in writing and speech within one country and yet, we are often divided by a common language. This is the more so from one country to another and in interpretation where much can be lost or confused in translation.

The purpose of this section is not to offer authoritative definitions of individual words and phrases for our discussions, but to explore sense and meaning. For each of us we should first assess if, in the descriptions offered, we find recognition and thereafter consider two further aspects.

- Are the words, referred to, and which largely appear in the "Key Principles and Challenges of Governance" section that follows, relevant to the interests of state or institution?
- Secondly, if they are, how fully are they applied in those differing contexts?

This section was prepared to engender greater debate and thought regarding governance issues.

The "Key Principles and Challenges of Governance" section refers to the aspects that will influence states in their approach to governance and autonomy. That section, also in the context of an autonomous governing body, describes that body as being the custodian of the values, purpose, and mission of the institution and of it being both autonomous and accountable.

It is suggested that the expanded meaning of the preceding sentence is that a governing body in the context of considerable autonomy should be a constantly vigilant guard of the values of the institution. Foremost of these should be academic freedom. No third party should dictate what may be taught or how, although obligations imposed by national and/or state statute will require to be considered. Further placing the individual learner at the heart of the institution's purpose should be of critical importance. Additional values of diversity, equality, and fairness are likely to be essential components of an institution's approach.

An autonomous institution will have the right of self-determination and self-government. This translates easily into ensuing its governing body should not be dictated to by third parties either in the composition of that body or as to how it should act.

This does not mean, of course, that the institution through its governing body need not be most responsive and accountable to the legitimate demands of stakeholders be they government, staff, students, sponsors, and so forth. These demands will relate both to learning expectations and outcomes as well as outcomes from funding imperatives.

Once constituted with autonomy the governing body should operate as a unitary board with a chair empowered both to be an advocate beyond the institution with third parties and to lead in holding the principal and his/her team to account.

Similarly, with such a structure and approach it is for the governing body to oversee the creation and delivery of the strategic direction of the institution that will, of course, encompass its purpose and mission. How such strategy is converted into detailed business planning is very much the responsibility of the principal and the executive, but must be delivered consistent with the values, purpose and mission of the institution.

In all of this the consequence of the autonomy, be it full or quasi, of an institution is the accountability of the governing body to stakeholders and others in having and claiming such autonomy. In this, members of a governing body require to understand with clarity where the legal, ethical and reputational accountabilities lie both for the governing body and for the individual member of that body. Likewise, the dividing line between the accountability of the governing body and the principal and executive must be crystal clear, dictating a well-crafted schedule of delegation to the principal and beyond. This will be required, even although in most circumstances the governing body will remain vicariously liable.

Finally, both in regard to the values of the institution and in the standards of the governing body collectively and for individual members there needs to be a clear commitment to the values of honesty, integrity, lack of self interest, and rejection of corrupt practices. These words should not need further elucidation, and again must apply both in the context of full and/or quasi autonomy.

The *Learning Forum* provided a useful arena in which these essential and uncompromising standards were expanded upon further.

Key Principles and Challenges of Governance[2]

This section seeks briefly to reflect upon aspects of governance of HEIs from both the perspective of the state and the individual institution. It does not attempt to be definitive, but offers a reflection of those issues that influence the attitudes of state legislators and at the other extreme key principles for governance of an autonomous institution.

The State Position

Introduction

Across the world many states have, over recent years, sought to balance demands for greater institutional autonomy with a need to direct strategic economic development, stimulate social engineering and enhance participation. Few challenge the national advantage in states rating well in OECD rankings regarding higher education and other tables, let alone individual institutions scoring highly in international league tables. The tension which exists is how best for states to facilitate progression in one of the most internationally competitive areas of the decade.

Models range from strict state control of institutions with no external funding to market dominated approaches. At either end of such a scale universities, as never before are at the center of national economic and social endeavor. Even with almost complete autonomy where institutions operate in the private sector, the state retains a direct interest, for example, in research, participation numbers, the quality of teaching and learning, and the relevance of graduates for the work place. If these interests are met according to the national policy of the day the state will be more inclined to relinquish direct or indirect controls.

There is a debate in many countries about the governance and management of higher education, and the relationship of institutions to the state. Many consider that the "grip of the state" has to be relaxed so that institutions can determine their own strategies and take more responsibility for their own financial sustainability. Corresponding changes in governance and accountability of HEIs are needed to support this changed relationship. This process has reached different points in many countries, but there is a common direction of travel.

The result of this process is that governments are less clearly seen as the "sole owner and core funder" of HEIs and so their ability to ensure policy objectives and financial sustainability becomes less direct.

This combination of factors leads to a number of challenges for policy makers, including:

- How can they ensure that increasingly autonomous institutions will deliver the government's education and social policy agenda?
- How can they ensure that financial incentives introduced for policy purposes do not cause HEIs to act suboptimally—reducing diversity and responsibility and perhaps threatening their own financial sustainability?
- How can they ensure that the public interest is adequately represented?
- How can they reduce the risk that a more autonomous and market-driven university system will become financially unstable and make further demands on the state if institutions get into difficulties?

Governance is an important issue that spans both the policy agenda and the institutional financial and management agenda. Governance arrangements can play an important part in the way that institutions are held accountable to the government and the public interest. They can also help institutions to ensure a coherent strategy and a sustainable development path.[3]

System Steering

Steering involves the means by which governments encourage the institutional components of a national system to function in order to link higher education to a country's strategic goals. Steering incentives can be direct and indirect, and include regulatory, structural, financial, contractual and competitive mechanisms. The balance between direct and indirect means often reflects the maturity of a nation's political economy, the strength of its HEIs, and the compatibility of institutional and governmental values.

Steering has been defined as "the externally derived instruments and institutional arrangements that seek to govern organisational and academic behaviours within HEIs."[4] The term suggests a less interventionist and more facilitative role for the state, whereby the state defines national goals, sets the structure of incentives, uses a variety of instruments to influence institutional behavior and performance, and monitors outcomes. The use of policy instruments and the monitoring of their effectiveness can be at arm's-length from government, such as through a 'buffer body' like the Higher Education Funding Council for England.

The most difficult challenge is striking the right balance at the right times in a country's progress, particularly the balance between government regulation and market mechanisms, between centralization and decentralization of decision-making, and between direct and indirect means of steering. This challenge also involves designing regulatory, financing and accountability instruments that fit the circumstances and help achieve national goals without stifling institutional innovation and differentiation.

The Institutional Position

Institutional Governance

Governance refers not so much to what institutions do but how they do it; the ways and means by which an institution sets its directions and organizes itself to fulfill its purpose. Governance can be understood generally to involve "the distribution of authority and functions among the units within a larger entity, the modes of communication and control among them, and the conduct of relationships between the entity and the surrounding environment."[5]

In higher education, governance processes deal with multiple dimensions of an institution: how it coheres; how its exercises authority; how it relates to internal members (students and staff); how it relates to external stakeholders (government, business, local community, international institutions); how it makes decisions; and how and how far it delegates responsibility for decisions and actions internally. The structure of governance includes the role of institutional governing boards and presidents, their participative structures, their procedural rules and sanctions, their policies for resource allocation, and their arrangements for performance management, monitoring and reporting.

Good governance facilitates decision-making which is rational, informed, and transparent, and which leads to organizational efficiency and effectiveness. An important characteristic of good governance is that of probity. Decision-making should ensure that varying interests are appropriately balanced, that the reasons behind competing interests are recognized, and that one interest is not endorsed over others on arbitrary grounds.[6]

A central consideration is the relationship of institutional governance to the state, primarily the extent of institutional autonomy and its effect on institutional performance. Institutions necessarily have to develop new capacities for internal governance when the locus of responsibility for decisions about student admission, staffing, curriculum, and the use of financial resources is shifted to the institutional level. An interesting policy question arises in respect of managing such a transition: should the devolution of responsibilities await demonstration of an institution's capacity to manage them, or does the capacity to manage increased responsibilities only develop once they are devolved?

Neave and van Vught portray a continuum in the relationship of government to HEIs from a "state control" model to a "state supervising" model;[7] that is a shift from intervening to influencing, or from "rowing" to "steering," or from micro-regulation to meta-regulation. Fielden suggests that this shift is made necessary by the larger scale and complexity of contemporary higher education systems:

> The management of very complex academic communities cannot be done effectively by remote civil servants, and the task should be left to institutions themselves. Giving them autonomy recognizes that their management needs are different and allows them full exercise of their academic freedoms. The constraints of centrally managing a system that needs to be flexible and responsive have become clear.[8]

The Interaction of System Steering with Institutional Autonomy, Accountability and Responsiveness

A useful distinction can be made between "substantive" autonomy and "procedural" (or operational) autonomy.[9] Substantive autonomy refers to the authority of institutions to determine academic and research policy including what and how to teach, whom to admit as students, whom to employ and promote in academic staffing appointments, what to research and publish, and the awarding of degrees.

Procedural autonomy refers to the authority of institutions in essentially non-academic areas such as revenue raising and expenditure management, non-academic staff appointments, purchasing, and entering into contracts. Procedural autonomy includes the freedom of an institution to manage its administrative affairs and expend the financial resources at its disposal in a prudent way to give effect to its priorities.[10]

"Accountability" is the flip side of the autonomy coin. It is the responsibility that an institution assumes in return for the freedom accorded it. Different dimensions of accountability can be illustrated by the basic questions: Who is accountable to whom, for what purposes, for whose benefit, by what means, and with what consequences?[11]

There are around the world a variety of autonomous or quasi-autonomous models of governance. The following describes key principles that underpin roles and responsibilities, and conduct and standards of governing bodies for an autonomous institution that has unambiguous responsibility for its strategic direction and execution in the hands of its governing body.

Role and Responsibilities

The governing body of a higher education institution acts as custodian of the values, purpose and mission of the institution. The values, purpose and mission of that institution are formulated by the governing body after wide consultation and upon the recommendation of the Principal on behalf of the executive.

Such values, purpose and mission should be owned by the governing body and the executive, be clearly described and widely publicized.

As such custodian, the governing body should assert the autonomy of and consequential accountability of the institution to all stakeholders.

The governing body should be unambiguously and collectively responsible for overseeing the institution's activities, determining its future direction and should foster an environment in which the institutional mission can be achieved allowing the potential of all learners connected to the institution to be maximized.

The chair of the governing body is responsible for the leadership of that body and has ultimate responsibility for its effectiveness. The chair has a particular responsibility for effective communication with stakeholders. The principal, as chief executive of the institution, is responsible for advice to the governing body in relation to strategic direction and is accountable to the governing body for the effective management of the institution. There needs to be absolute clarity in the distinction between the governance function of the governing body and the executive responsibilities of the principal and the executive team led by him or her.

Conduct and Standards

There should be a balance of skill and experience amongst members of the governing body sufficient to enable it to meet its primary responsibilities and to ensure stakeholder confidence, particularly that of government and its agencies.

Individual members and governing bodies collectively should at all times conduct themselves honestly, with integrity, lack of self-interest and without engaging in corrupt practices. All members should exercise their responsibilities in the best interests of the institution as a whole rather than for personal gain or as a representative of any narrow interest group.

The governing body should keep its own effectiveness under regular review and should use objective measurement to determine that effectiveness using for instance key performance indicators and wherever possible benchmarking institutional performance against comparable institutions.

New members of a governing body should receive a full induction upon joining the governing body and during membership of that body should be willing to receive training and development to ensure that the member has the necessary skills and knowledge to discharge effectively his or her responsibilities as a member of the governing body.

Conclusion

As stated in a 2004 OECD report:

> As higher education has grown, and other pressures have constrained state funding, the financial sustainability of universities and other institutions of higher education has become an issue for policy makers, and for those who govern and manage these institutions.
>
> The challenge for governments is to ensure that increasingly autonomous and market-driven institutions respond to public interest agendas, at national and regional levels, while also taking a greater responsibility for their own financial, academic and management sustainability. The challenge for institutions is to manage a more complex portfolio of aims and funding; to differentiate themselves in

an increasingly competitive environment; and to protect and maintain academic quality and their ability to deliver over the long term.[12]

Accountability (in the policy sense) is a necessary corollary to autonomy. The factors that drive in the direction of autonomy also make it necessary to establish new mechanisms to ensure that institutions are responsive to the national and regional public interest; and to the needs of different stakeholder groups.

Good governance facilitates decision-making that is rational, informed, and transparent, which leads to organizational efficiency and effectiveness that supports and fosters the development of high-quality education and research.

The purpose of this section is to stimulate reflection. It is hoped that readers will consider from their standpoint, be that from a state or institutional perspective, if they, at this stage, favor the status quo granting or seeking greater autonomy to or from institutions or restricting it and for what reason.

Notes

[1] By Andrew Cubie, Chair of the Court of Napier University, The Scottish and Credit and Qualification Framework, and former Chair of the University Chairs of the UK.

[2] By Andrew Cubie, Chair of the Court of Napier University, The Scottish and Credit and Qualification Framework, and former Chair of the University Chairs of the UK; and Aims McGuinness, Senior Associate of the National Center for Higher Education Management Systems (NCHEMS) in the United States and former chair of the Board of Trustees of the State Colleges in Colorado.

[3] OECD On the Edge: Securing a Sustainable Future for Higher Education Report 2004.

[4] Ferlie, E., Musselin, C. and Andresani, G. (2007), "The 'Steering' of Higher Education Systems: A Public Management Perspective," Paper prepared for the ESF project *Higher Education Looking Forward* (HELF), Brussels.

[5] Ricci., A. (1999) "College and University Governance in the United States: An Historical Survey." [http://www.newfoundations.com/History/HEGovernance.html].

[6] Trakman, L. (2008) "Modelling University Governance." *Higher Education Quarterly* **62**, 1/2, 63-83.

[7] Neave, G., and van Vught. F. A. (1994) *Government and Higher Education Relationships Across Three Continents.* Oxford: Pergamon Press.

[8] Fielden. J. (2008), "Global Trends in University Governance." Education Working paper Series, Number 9. The World Bank, March.

[9] Berdahl, R. (1990) "Academic Freedom, Autonomy and Accountability in British Universities." *Studies in Higher Education.* Vol. 15.

[10] Government of India, Ministry of Human Resource Development (2005). *Report of the Central Advisory Board of Education (CABE) Committee on Autonomy of Higher Education Institutions.* (Kanti Biswas Report). Delhi, June 2005, p. 21.

[11] Burke, J. (2004). "The Many Faces of Accountability." *Achieving Accountability in Higher Education: Balancing Public, Academic, and Market Demands.* Burke, J and Associates, eds., San Francisco: Jossey-Bass, p. 2.

[12] OECD (2004) *On the Edge: Securing a Sustainable Future for Higher Education* Geneva: OECD.

CHAPTER 3

State Case Studies

*State Governments of Andhra Pradesh,
Haryana, Karnataka, and West Bengal*

Andhra Pradesh[1]

Section One: Context, Size and Shape of the Higher Education Sector

Higher Education in the State of Andhra Pradesh is looked after by the government under the Department of Higher Education. While the Commissionerate of Technical Education deals with the Polytechnic, Engineering, Architecture, Pharmacy, MBA, and MCA education, the Commissionerate of Collegiate Education deals with post 10+2 programs in general education.

Andhra Pradesh State Council for Higher Education (APSCHE) constituted through a State Act[2] in 1988, as per National Education Policy 1986 is first of its kind in India. APSCHE coordinates, and liaises between University Grants Commission, the state government, and Universities. There were 32 State Universities, 9 Deemed Universities, and 3 Central Universities in the state during 2008–09.[3] The State Governor is the Chancellor of most of the universities and the Vice-Chancellor (a senior academician) of the university is appointed by the state government.

The university constituent colleges affiliated self-financing private colleges offer undergraduate/postgraduate and M. Phil and Ph.D. programs. Besides university constituent colleges there are Government Degree Colleges totally funded by the government.

About 45 percent of the existing colleges in Andhra Pradesh are professional colleges offering Engineering, Medicine, Pharmacy, Agriculture, Veterinary, MBA, and MCA programs. Forty-three percent of student population in higher education goes for professional education.

The lone technological university existing hitherto in the state is divided into Jawaharlal Nehru Technological University Hyderabad, Ananthapur, and Kakinada and Jawaharlal Nehru University for Architecture, and Fine Arts, Hyderabad in the year 2007–08. These universities affiliate engineering, technology, pharmacy, architecture, and management institutions.

During the last couple of years, tremendous growth has been observed in professional institutions providing increased access to technical education. The growth is more in the private sector while some university engineering colleges have also come up. Density of these institutions is more in urban and semiurban areas. There are 628 engineering institutions in the state with an annual intake of 216,280 for the academic year 2009–10.

The Andhra Pradesh (Regulation of Admissions, and Prohibition of Capitation Fee) Act 1983 governs the admissions into professional colleges. Admissions into the professional colleges are through common entrance tests (EAMCET, ECET (FDH), ICET, LAWCET, PGCET and so forth) conducted under the aegis of APSCHE with weightage for qualifying exam in certain courses. Eighty-five percent of available seats in professional colleges are reserved for local candidates belonging to Andhra, Sri Venkateshwara, and Osmania university regions as per presidential order.[4] One third of the seats are reserved for women candidates in all professional courses. Other statutory reservations[5] in favor of scheduled castes (SC), scheduled tribes (ST), and backwards castes (BC) candidates also exist. Since 2008, 5 percent of seats have been reserved in favor of Muslim minority candidates. The tuition fee is fixed by the Admission and Fee Regulatory Committee[6] (AFRC). The average pass percentage in technical education is near the national average of 65 percent.

The funding to the state universities is on a block grant pattern by providing the total salary component by the state government, while the university/constituent colleges retain their tuition fee for meeting the other recurring, and nonrecurring costs. The private institutions are funded by student tuition fees.

Except the universities established during the last 3–4 years, all other universities are NAAC accredited and the eight constituent engineering colleges have sought NBA accreditation. There are 93 degree and 5 diploma institutions accredited[7] by NBA in the state.

Engineering and technical education became highly popular in the state for the well-known reason of high employment potential in India, and abroad, which resulted in high enrollment in all institutions except in some branches. It is a matter of deep concern that enrollment in basic sciences is alarmingly coming down. The state reimburses tuition fee and provides maintenance charges to all the students, irrespective of their category, whose annual parental income is up to Rs. 100,000 in all post-secondary education institutions, in the state. The state also provides Prathiba Scholarships to meritorious students.

Section Two: Specific Governance Arrangements

State Government Higher Education Department
- Establishes state universities through an act of the state legislature
- Receives policy support in planning, co-ordination, and academic functions in higher education from APSCHE
- Provides block grant to state universities and their constituent colleges (covering the entire salary component and a part of other expenditure)
- Provides 100 percent funding to government institutions offering higher education including polytechnic education.
- State government representatives (Principal Secretary of Higher Education Department, Commissioners of Technical Education/Collegiate Education) are on the Executive Council of Universities
- Does not interfere in academic activities of the universities
- Permits the establishment of new self-financing private professional institutions after the approval given by the respective central regulatory agencies (MCI, AICTE, PCI, CoA, NC, NCTE and so forth).

Table 3.1. Number, Type, and Intake of Higher Education Institutions

Sr. No	Category	Type of Institution	No. of Institutions			Intake		
			Government Aided	Private	Total	Government Aided	Private	Total
1.	Degree Level Courses/ Institutions	Engineering College(BE)	8	133	141	2,485	40,220	42,705
2.		Pharmacy Colleges(BPHARM)	4	28	32	225	1,695	1,920
3.		Hotel Management Colleges (BHMCT)	—	05	05	—	300	300
		Subtotal	12	166	178	2,710	42,215	44,925
4.	PG Level Course/ Institute	MCA Colleges	5	49	54	345	2,895	3,240
5.		MBA Colleges	8	149	157	780	11,825	12,605
		Subtotal	13	198	211	3,835	14,720	15,845
6.	Diploma Level Courses/Institutions	Polytechnics	39	111	150	17,460	31,620	49,080
		Total	64	475	539	21,295	88,555	109,850

Source: State Government of Andhra Pradesh.

State Universities

- Exercise full autonomy with accountability
- Act independently as per their respective executive council decisions
- Receive block grant from state government and different type of funds from other funding agencies like UGC, AICTE, DST and so forth
- Retain tuition and other fees and generate revenues through consultancy and so forth
- Totally accountable for the budget provided, academic standards, and performance
- Run constituent colleges and some of them are autonomous
- Affiliate private self-financing institutions, provide them curriculum for approved courses, conduct exams, award degrees, and conduct academic audits
- Seek NAAC accreditation from time to time.

Deemed Universities

- No public grants
- Sustain with self funding that is,
  - through fees (uncontrolled), which is usually higher than what is fixed by AFRC
  - Other charges collected for support services
- Run courses of their choice, curriculum, and conduct examinations, and award degrees (constraints—uncontrolled fee structure and admissions, standards not comparable with university engineering colleges).

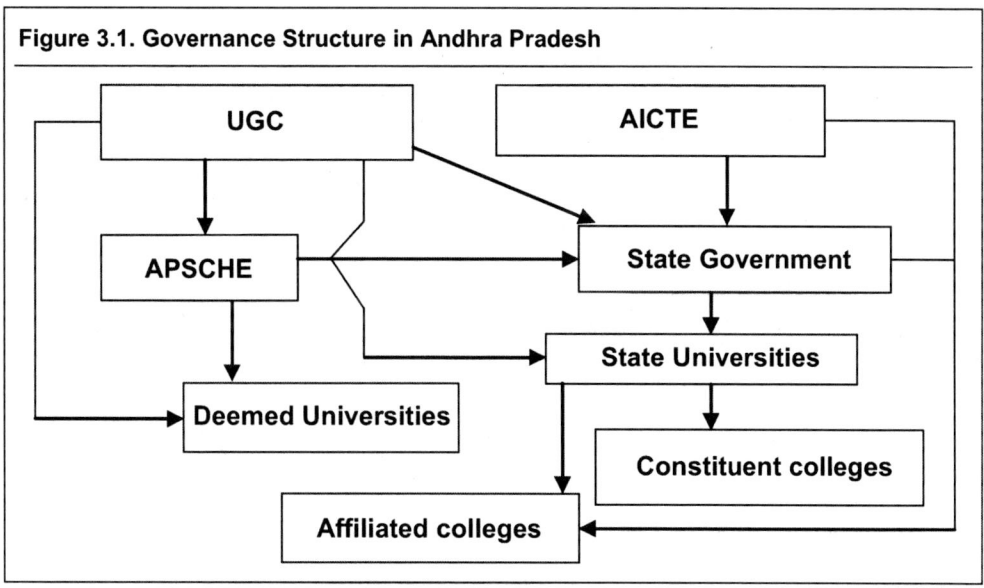

Figure 3.1. Governance Structure in Andhra Pradesh

Source: State Government of Andhra Pradesh.

Affiliated Private Institutions
- Seek approvals from AICTE and affiliation from university regularly and run only approved courses
- No regular government grants (receive grants only in special circumstances like TEQIP, and from AICTE for research and other activities)
- Self sustaining through tuition and other fees as fixed by AFRC
- Institutions are eligible to collect Rs. 3,000 more per year in addition to tuition fee for the accredited programs
- Curriculum, examinations, and award of degrees is done by affiliating university
- Enjoy autonomy except in academic matters
- Accountable in the matters of collection of fees, academic works, quality issues, and all other regulatory requirements.

Section Three: Recent Reforms
- Rationalization[8] of faculty in universities
- Empowered 12 TEQIP institutions[9] to exercise autonomy with accountability, promoted improvement of governance capacity, created academic excellence, developed networking concept for resource sharing and enhancement of outreach of services to community

- Increased concern on quality among the affiliated colleges resulting in more number of NBA accredited institutions in the state
- Enabled the meritorious poor and deprived (whose annual income is less than Rs. 100,000 per year) class of students belonging to SC/ST/BC/Minority/EBC categories to join professional courses by government paying their tuition fees.
- Vice chancellors forum started to deliberate and take action on important common issues.

Section Four: Lessons for Other Indian States or Other Countries

- Provided increased access to Technical Education, and facilitated almost total enrollment by way of exemption of tuition fees for the poor and at affordable cost for others.
- Successful completion of TEQIP by providing right policy support.
- Drafted initiatives of the state on the recommendations of the National Knowledge Commission by the Department of Technical Education emphasizing issues on faculty development, teaching-learning processes, examination, and evaluation system and industry-institution interaction.
- APSCHE for policy support and coordination: Assists in planning and coordination in the matters of starting new higher education institutions, developmental programs, determination, and maintenance of educational standards, promote cooperation, and coordination for resource sharing among institutions, increase scope for industry interaction and suggest ways, and means of augmenting additional resources in universities and colleges.
- Creation of state universities (32): The state has created universities in almost all the districts for efficient monitoring of HEIs including oriental colleges in the state.
- Starting new university engineering colleges (19): During the last 2 to 3 years the numbers of university engineering colleges have been doubled in the state for increased accessibility of high-quality technical education for meritorious deprived section of higher secondary passouts at affordable costs established in unrepresented areas and specializations in the state.
- Rajiv Gandhi University of Knowledge Technology[10] (RGUKT) established in 2008 for meritorious rural youth of AP. The three IIITs (International Institutes of Information Technology) which are totally residential are governed by an independent University Governing Council under RGUKT. These institutes are specialized in teaching, and research in IT and other emerging disciplines. The annual intake in each IIIT is 2000 with 65 percent of seats for rural mandal school pass outs. The programs offered are of six years duration leading to B.Tech in IT and a B.Tech or M.Sc in one of the other domain specialization in engineering sciences and social sciences

Table 3.1. Growth of Technical Institutions in Andhra Pradesh from 1996–97 to 2008–09

Sl. No.	YEAR	Engineering		B.Pharmacy		MBA		MCA		Polytechnics	
		No. of Coll.	No.of Seats	No.of Coll.	No.of Seats	No.of Coll.	No.of Seats	No.of Coll.	No.of Seats	No.of Coll.	No.of Seats
1	1996–97	37	10,455	6	310	57	2,145	44	1,330	93	14,190
2	1997–98	57	14,155	20	890	81	3,000	75	2,270	94	15,850
3	1998–99	89	19,773	21	970	92	3,825	99	3,020	100	16,705
4	1999–00	102	25,064	24	1,190	109	4,660	153	4,890	103	17,580
5	2000–01	107	30,896	24	1,190	110	4,680	162	6,395	103	17,860
6	2001–02	174	46,090	26	1,390	143	7,274	236	10,075	104	19,410
7	2002–03	217	62,710	28	1,510	160	9,039	263	12,795	104	19,410
8	2003–04	225	65,960	31	1,770	207	11,370	272	12,865	120	21,210
9	2004–05	238	82,225	55	3,240	217	13,525	313	17,225	140	22,635
10	2005–06	262	92,600	82	4,850	220	13,755	293	16,540	141	22,965
11	2006–07	282	98,793	112	6,215	197	17,189	237	21,415	142	23,860
12	2007–08	337	118,993	225	13,319	194 (368)	26,228	281 (480)	31,869	146	25,000
13	2008–09	530	174,742	254	15,155	*224 (454)	32,598	*370 (653)	44,485	213	63,075

* Standalone Colleges

MBA Stand Alone	224	18,840
MBA offered in Engineering Colleges	168	10,038
MBA offered in MCA Colleges	62	3,720
TOTAL	454	32,598

MCA Stand Alone	370	27,505
MCA offered in Engineering Colleges	232	13,920
MCA offered in MBA Colleges	51	3,060
TOTAL	653	44,485

Source: State Government of Andhra Pradesh.

Haryana[11]

Section One: Context, Size, and Shape of the Higher Education Sector

Technical and professional manpower is the most important component of human resources for socioeconomic development of the state. The Department of Technical Education prepares the technical managers, scientists, engineers, supervisors, and other professionals including skilled technicians through post graduate/under graduate and diploma level institutions in the fields of Engineering and Technology, Computer Science, IT, Management, Pharmacy, Architecture, Hotel Management, and Applied Arts and Crafts. Particularly, during the second half of the 10th Five Year Plan and the current (11th) Five Year Plan, capacity expansion has more than doubled. The 11th Five Year Plan targets of intake of 50,000 at undergraduate level, 50,000 at diploma level, and 50,000 at skill level are expected to be achieved during 2009–10, that is, much before the closure of the 11th Five Year Plan.

At the time of inception of Haryana as a separate state in 1966, there were only six polytechnics and only one engineering college at Kurukshetra (all government/government aided) with annual intake of 1,341 approximately. As othe number of institutions has been increased to 539 with an annual intake of 109,850.

During the last five years, there has been exponential growth of technical institutions in the state. The enrollment of students every year has increased manifold. In the year 2004–05, there were only 145 technical institutes offering diploma and degree programs with an intake of 24,124, which has currently increased to 539 institutions with intake of more than 100,000, an increase of nearly 450 percent. Similarly, the budget of the department has increased greatly during last five years from Rs. 29 crore in 2004–05 to Rs. 315 crore for the current year.

Today the ratio of availability of professional seats to the total population in the state is one of the highest in the country. As per the current statistics, there is one degree level institution against 138,000 of population, one PG-level institution per 116,000 of population and one diploma level institution per 163,000 of population. There is one seat in degree level courses per 545 of the population, one seat in PG courses per 1,546 of the population and one seat in diploma level courses per 500 of population.

Degree Engineering/PG Education

- 2004–05: 114 degree/PG institutions: annual intake of 16,945
- 2009–10: The number of institutions grew to 389 (25 government/ government aided + 364 private); annual intake 56,935.
- CR State College of Engineering, Murthal (Government Engineering College) upgraded in year 2006 to Deenbandhu Chhotu Ram University of Science, and Technology, Murthal with a view to greater autonomy.
- Guru Jambheshwar University, Hisar converted to Guru Jambheshwar University of Science and Technology, Hisar with a view to introducing more innovation and research-oriented Science and technology programs.
- YMCA Institute of Engineering, Faridabad (a government-aided engineering college) upgraded in 2009 to the level of university with a view to give greater autonomy.

- Ch. Devi Lal Memorial Engineering College, Panniwala Mota (a government engineering college) made a constituent college/faculty of Ch. Devi Lal University, Sirsa.
- Three private engineering colleges (M.M. Engineering College, Mullana (Ambala), Lingay's Institute of Mgt., and Tech., Faridabad and Manav Rachna College of Engineering, Faridabad) upgraded to the level of deemed universities as per the Haryana Private Universities Act 2006 and UGC Act.
- The policy of granting autonomy to the well performing institutions notified by the government in the year 2007. Two private engineering colleges— namely Institute of Technology, and Management, Gurgaon and NC College of Engineering Israna (Panipat) affiliated with MDU Rohtak, and Kurukshetra University Kurukshetra respectively—have been declared autonomous under autonomy policy.
- Indian Institute of Management is being established at Rohtak. The first class is likely to start in 2010–11.
- Indian Institute of Information Technology is proposed to be setup at Sonipat.
- Four state-of-the-art institutes, namely: State Institute of Fashion Design, State Institute of Film, and Television, State Institute of Fine Arts, and State Institute of Professional Studies are being established at Rohtak. These institutions shall become operational in 2010–11.

Diploma (Polytechnic) Education

- In 2004–05, diploma institutions numbered 31 (21 government/government aided + 10 private) with annual intake of 7,179. In the year 2009–10 the number of institutions grew to 150 (39 government/government aided + 111 private) with annual intake of 49,080.
- To provide greater autonomy and more stability of staff, the governance in four existing government polytechnics has been converted into societal mode, wherein the governance of the polytechnic is through BOG. All the new government polytechnics are being established in societal mode. Until 2005 there were only 16 government polytechnics. From 2006 onwards 13 government polytechnics have been established and all are functioning under societal mode.
- Double shift has been introduced in nine government polytechnics for capacity expansion and optimal utilization of resources.
- Six Centers of Excellence have been established from the year 2009–10: in the area of Plastic Technology at Government Polytechnic, Mechatronics at Government Polytechnic, Nilokheri, Chemical Engineering at Government Polytechnic, Sonepat, Automobile Engineering at Government Polytechnic Manesar, Ceramic Engineering at Government Polytechnic, Jhajjar), Textile Technology at Government Polytechnic, Hisar.
- Central Institute of Plastic Engineering and Technology is being established on the campus of Deenbandhu Chhotu Ram University of Science, and Technology, Murthal (Sonipat).

- Education through satellite under the EDUSAT Project of Government of India has started from the year 2006. All government polytechnics have been covered under the scheme.

Other Projects/Activities Concerning Higher Education

- A Central University has been established at Jaat Pali in Mahindergarh Distt.
- Rajiv Gandhi Education City is being set up at Kundli in Distt, Sonipat. The institutions of excellence for higher learning/research are proposed to be setup in Education City. Nine applicants having collaboration with renowned foreign universities/institutions/industries have recently been allotted land in Education City.
- The first women's university, namely Bhagat Phool Singh Mahila University, has been established at Khanpur Kalan (Sonipat).
- The Haryana Private Universities Act came into force in the year 2006, which shall provide for establishment and incorporation of private universities in the State of Haryana for imparting higher education and to regulate their functions and for matters connected therewith. Three private engineering colleges have been granted the status of university under provisions of this act.

Other Activities

The state IRG Scheme has been notified and implemented to encourage consultancy by the faculty. The salient features of the IRG policy are as follows:

- Fifteen percent overheads to the cost estimates; these shall go to the revenue head
- Consultancy project using institutional infrastructure: 50 percent to institution and 50 percent to faculty
- Consultancy project without using institutional infrastructure: 30 percent to institution and 70 percent to faculty
- Institution share shall go to the development fund of the institute
- Net revenue shall be after meeting all expenses incurred on raw material, stationery, hospitality, out sourcing of manpower, and remitting the 15 percent over head charges to the revenue
- Curriculum and academic calendar have been made uniform for all the institutions
- Credit based system has been introduced in government engineering colleges
- Technical audit of labs in government polytechnics has been conducted through professional agencies
- SWOT analysis has been done by the National Institute of Technical Teachers' Training and Research for all government polytechnics
- Students charter enforced in all institutions.

Section Two: Specific Governance Arrangements

The major functions of the Technical Education Department are as follows:

- To promote and develop technical education in the state by:

- Starting new courses in emerging new technologies with the approval of AICTE
- Opening new institutions in state to expand training facilities, with the approval of AICTE
- Providing infrastructural facilities to the institutions functioning under the aegis of the department

- To formulate educational policies and programs and disseminate the policies of the government with respect to Technical Education System
- To plan annual budget allocation for technical education in state and ensure optimal utilization of funds
- To ensure standards of technical standards by facilitating provision of state of art quality education and training in areas of technical and technician education
- To monitor the standards of institutions and initiate corrective measures
- To prescribe rules of recruitment, promotion for faculty
- To implement World Bank Assisted Project
- To promote entrepreneurship development
  - Develop strong linkages with industries
  - Continuous staff development
  - Facilitate networking and collaboration amongst the institutions in the state.

Two autonomous entities—Haryana State Counseling Society and Haryana State Board of Technical Education—have been created under the department for smooth performance of the functions of the department. The Haryana State Counseling Society is responsible for implementation of transparent and uniform policies regarding admissions. It is the nodal agency for carrying out online admissions to all AICTE approved technical courses in the state. The Haryana State Board of Technical Education is responsible for coordinated development of technical education in diploma level institutes (polytechnics), which includes examination, curricula, industry institute interaction, placement, development of learning resources, and other related academic activities.

Budget

- The approved outlay for the Technical Education Department for the 11th Five Year Plan (2007-12) is Rs. 67,300 lacs (US$145.2 million). For the year 2009–10 an outlay of Rs. 15,790 and 15,771 lacs (US$34.1 million) has been approved under Plan and Non-Plan Schemes respectively. The budget of the department has increased ten-fold from 2004–05 to Rs. 315 crores (US$67.9 million) in 2009–10.

Quality Assurance

- Assessment and accreditation of institution and programs is being done mainly by the two national agencies (i) the National Assessment and Accreditation Council (NAAC) set up by UGC and (ii) the National Board of Accreditation (NBA) setup by AICTE.

■ Besides accreditation by national agencies, the state government on its own is now more focused on providing quality in technical institutes. The state government has initiated introduction of credit based scheme, notification of students charter and inter-se grading, and ISO certification of all technical Institutes, intro. The state has also empanelled three agencies for inter-se-grading of technical institutions. Quality certification has been made mandatory.

Section Three: Recent Reforms Related to Governance

Reforms under TEQIP

The institutions have been empowered through grant of full academic, financial, administrative, and managerial autonomy and further by implementation of the Block Grant Scheme and establishment of the Corpus Fund, Staff Development Fund, Depreciation/Renewal Fund, and Maintenance Fund. This has helped the institutions to manage their own affairs. Under the Block Grant Scheme institutions have the following kinds of autonomy:

■ Allocate/re-allocate the block grant to expenditure category as they deem best serves to the institution
■ Retain revenue generated at the institute level without reduction in government funding and to use generated revenue for institutional development and maintenance
■ Enhance revenue generation by various means within the broad mandate of the institute
■ Determine terms of employment (duration, wage, benefits and so forth.) of faculty and staff
■ To redistribute faculty and staff positions in different cadre
■ To redesign job profile based on their requirements
■ Employ additional faculty and staff on contract to meet requirements with the block grant available
■ Take fiscal decision for better financial management of the institution
■ The institutions are now governed by their own BOG with adequate representation from the stakeholders including industry, faculty, parents and students
■ Institutional management has been decentralized with delegation of financial and decision-making powers to various functionaries. The financial powers of the Director have been enhanced to Rs. 100,000, and senior functionaries/HODs to Rs. 10,000.

Other Reforms

The policy of granting autonomy to the well performing institutions notified by the state government in the year 2007. Two private engineering colleges have been declared autonomous under the autonomy policy: the Institute of Technology and Management, Gurgaon and the NC College of Engineering Israna (Panipat). They are affiliated with MDU Rohtak and Kurukshetra University Kurukshetra respectively. An autonomous institute under the policy has been granted the freedom to:

■ Determine and prescribe its own course of study, restructure and redesign the course to suit the local needs/needs of industry, design and develop research based courses, integrated courses and value-added technical courses

■ Prescribe rules for admission in consonance with the reservation policy of the state

■ Evolve methods of assessment of student's performance, the conduct of examinations an notification of results

■ Use modern tools of educational technology to achieve higher standards and greater creativity

■ Promote practices such as community service, extension activities, projects for the benefits of the society at large, neighborhood programs, and so forth

■ Optimize the use of its infrastructure and facilities

■ Collaborate with leading national/international institutions/ organizations, to enhance its branch equity/ reputation as a top-of-the-line education provider.

To provide greater autonomy and more stability of staff, the governance in four existing government polytechnics has been converted into societal mode, wherein the governance of the polytechnic is through BOG. All the new government polytechnics are being established in societal mode. Until 2005 there were only 15 government polytechnics. Since 2006, 10 government polytechnics have been established and all are functioning under societal mode.

The Haryana State Counseling Society was set up in 2006 for carrying out the online admissions for all AICTE approved technical courses in the state. The state has received a "Golden Icon" Award from the Government of India and an "Excellence Award" from the Computer Society of India for online admissions.

Haryana State Board of Technical Education was set up in 2008 for coordinated development of diploma-level technical education in state. The main functions of the Board are to make all arrangements for smooth conduct and supervision of examinations, to deal with policy matters relating to teaching and training of the students and to grant affiliation to new institutions and new courses.

The State Fee Committee has been constituted under the chairmanship of Honorable Justice (Retired) of Punjab and Haryana High Court for fixation of fee in all technical institutions of the state. To set fees, the Committee takes into consideration the audited accounts statement and also look at the infrastructure development cost, academic cost, and other costs toward support services like hostel, sports, and so forth.

ICT infrastructure has been continually enhanced to improve transparency and accountability in the system such as on-line admissions, on-line entrance test, computerized MIS for the institutions, computerized performance appraisal of teachers by students, online sessional tests, campus wide networking, and so forth.

Social Sector Reforms

■ For girls: 25 percent horizontal reservation in admission, Rs. 5,100 cash award to every girl topper. Exemption of tuition fee in government/government aided polytechnics.

■ For minorities: 50 percent reservation in Government Polytechnic Uttawar for candidates of Mewat region and 50 percent reservation in Government

Polytechnic for Women, Morni for the candidates of Shivalik Development Board area.

■ For SC: Reimbursement of tuition fee, imparting pre-admission coaching, construction of 10 SC hostels imparting vocational educational programs in vocational education institutions through funding by the Social Welfare Department.

■ For physically handicapped: one percent reservation for physically handicapped candidates. In three polytechnics—GP Hisar/BPS, Mahila Khanpur/GP, and Sirsa—reservation of 75 seats for persons with disabilities under MHRD scheme with free education.

■ For Kashmiri migrants: Reservation of one seat in every branch in every institution. Fifty percent tuition fee concession.

■ For rural youth: reservation of one seat in each branch in diploma, and degree engineering in each institution for Haryana Government School Toppers.

■ For economically weaker sections and meritorious candidates: Scholarship amounting to Rs. 414.5 lacs provided by Haryana State Counseling Society in 2008–09 (917 candidates benefited). Tuition fee waiver scheme of AICTE implemented (6,000 seats created). Award of Rs. 10,000 to Haryana candidate scoring any of the first 10 ranks in national examination such as IIT/AIEEE/CAT/MAT.

Section Four: Lessons for Other Indian States or Other Countries

In the state where industrial development has taken a leap, the political leadership sensed the need for trained manpower and embarked upon the task. In the last five years, private sector investment to the tune of Rs. 5,000 crores has been crystallized in the technical education system. Besides an investment of Rs. 400 crores has been made by the government sector. National institutes like IIM, IIIT, and the Central Institute of Plastics Engineering and Technology are being set up. As per the trend of liberalized economy, the education system in the state is now more focused on decentralization of the powers. Institutes are now given more decision making and spending power. Many institutes have now been upgraded to autonomous status.

Good Governance Practices

■ Introduction of double shift in selected government polytechnics for optimal utilization of the resources. So far the double shift has been introduced in nine government polytechnics.

■ Conversion of governance from government mode to society mode (through BOG) in selected existing government polytechnics to provide greater autonomy. All new government polytechnics are being established in the societal mode.

■ Student's charter has been made mandatory for institutions, which is now part of the by-laws of the governing body of the institution.

■ Granting of autonomous status to the well performing institutions; the autonomy policy notified by the government in the year 2007. Under the policy, two private engineering colleges have been declared autonomous: the Institute of Technology and Management, Gurgaon and the NC College of

Engineering Israna (Panipat). They are affiliated with MDU Rohtak and Kurukshetra University Kurukshetra respectively.

- Empowered TEQIP institutions through grant of full academic, financial, administrative and managerial autonomy and further by implementation of Block Grant Scheme and, establishment of Corpus Fund, Staff Development Fund, Depreciation/Renewal Fund and Maintenance Fund. This has helped the institutions to manage their own affairs.
- Quality certification mandatory for all institutions.

Karnataka[12]

Section One: Context, Size, and Shape of the Higher Education Sector

The State of Karnataka:

- Pioneered reforms in technical education in the 1960s
- One of the early states to trigger quality technical education on large scale
- Karnataka has the largest pool of young talent in all disciplines
- No. of Engineering Colleges—178; No. of Polytechnics—274; No. of Industrial Training Institutes—629; No. of Job Oriented Course Centers—587

Intake of These Institutions—Annual Admissions

- Job Oriented Course Centers: 40,350 students
- Industrial Training Institutes: 137,494 students
- Diploma: 71,000+ students
- Undergraduate Engineering (B.E./B.Tech.) intake: 71,000+ students
- Post Graduate Engineering (M.E./M.Tech./MCA) intake: 4,500+ students
- Ph.D. enrollment: 1,400+

Academic Outputs of Faculty in Last Three Years in the State of Karnataka

- No. of journal publications: 1,500+ (80 percent of which would be in international journals)
- No. of conference publications: 4,000+ (70 percent of which would be international conferences)
- No. of patents obtained by faculty: 25+
- No. of books published by faculty: 240+
- No. of lab manuals developed by faculty: 400+
- No. of awards received by faculty: 170+
- No. of Ph.D.s awarded to scholars supervised by faculty: 180+
- Core competencies developed by interdepartmental and inter-institutional efforts: 25

Number of Networking Developments

Instances: Between institutions in Karnataka; between institutions in Karnataka and research organizations and industries all over India; and between institutions in India and universities in the United Kingdom, United States, Bangkok, and so forth.

- Joint workshops, training programs, conferences, faculty exchange: 400+
- Joint research undertaken: 60+
- Joint research publications between faculty of institutions: 550+

Industry-Higher Education Links

- No. of linkages: 200 +
- Faculty days in industry: 5000+
- Student days in industry: 60,000+
- No. of adjunct lectures: 700+

The link with Bosch Rexroth has resulted in establishment of state of the art training centers in hydraulics, pneumatics, sensorics, robotics—being used to train diploma and job-oriented course center students.

The link with GM has resulted in participation of several student groups in the design of an emerging market vehicle working with 18 universities across the globe

The link with Phillips has resulted in a full-fledged design lab in the campus with opportunities for students to work on and design to solve industrial grade real-life problems besides the opportunity to introduce industrial grade design software in the curriculum.

Section Two: Specific Governance Arrangements

- Admission policies—Government of Karnataka, Ministry of Higher Education
  - Qualifying exam requirements, common entrance test conduction, common admission to institutions across the state based on performance in common entrance test, and qualifying exam, quotas for rural students, women and tribals

- Fee fixation—Government of Karnataka
  - Based on fee fixation committee which studies the income-expenditure statements of institutions over previous years to fix fees

- Academic matters
  - State Technical University, the Visvesvaraya Technological University (VTU) for non-autonomous institutions regarding curriculum, lab requirements, faculty qualifications and cadres, conduction of examinations
  - Respective Academic Council for autonomous institutions

- Quality and compliance monitoring
  - All India Council for Technical Education (AICTE), a national statutory body, through annual approval procedures, mandatory disclosures and visits of nominated expert committees
  - The National Board of Accreditation on voluntary basis to assess institutions on several criteria such as teaching-learning processes, governance, research, faculty and student quality and achievements, and so forth
  - The University Grants Commission for granting autonomous status based on periodic inspections
  - The VTU through its annual affiliation processes to assess quality of teaching-learning process, compliance in terms of library, equipment, faculty and space
  - Government of Karnataka through SPFU, and the Directorate of Technical Education through its various approval and audit processes.

Mode of Operation
- Autonomy related approvals
  - The VTU recommends grant of autonomous status to its affiliated institutions based on criteria such as infrastructure, faculty position,

student results, accreditation status, and so forth subject to the concurrence of the UGC to the Government of Karnataka. The UGC inspects the institutions through an expert committee and grants autonomous status through a state government notification

- Compliance to academic norms such as faculty positions and cadres, faculty-student ratios, library requirements, equipment requirements, facilities for faculty and students, procedures for assessment and evaluation of students
  - VTU, AICTE, Academic Council on annual basis

- Compliance to infrastructural norms such as built area for instructional purposes, administrative purposes, circulation, recreation, labs, utility purposes, equipment, library, computers, and so forth
  - VTU, AICTE on annual basis.

Section Three: Recent Reforms Related to Governance

- Autonomy to institutions
  - Since 2007. Has resulted in greater accountability and responsibility of faculty. Curriculum has been restructured and revised with emphasis on analysis and design. Credit system has been adopted along with continuous internal evaluation, which has equal weight as the end semester end examination. Student performance has considerably increased
  - Adoption of credit based system with options of self-paced learning and regulations in place to handle exigencies

- BOG in place
  - Since 2004. Has resulted in greater de-centralization and delegation of powers and has led to creation of several bodies to look into issues such as quality assurance, financial matters, academic matters, grievances, recruitment, and so forth

- Delegation of powers to a HODs, faculty and various committees such as finance, planning, quality assurance, academic council, boards of studies, grievance cell, and so forth
  - Since institutions attained autonomous status in 2007. Led to more transparency and stake holder satisfaction as evident from various performance audits

- Large percentage of faculty trained in emerging areas
  - Since 2004, which has led to a surge in faculty research, no. of research papers, development of competencies in crucial areas of national interest such as structural design, ground engineering, VLSI design, signal processing

- Vibrant industry interaction leading to sponsored projects, research and consultancy
  - Since 2005 in terms of students being involved to solve live problems, industry setting up labs in institutions, adjunct faculty from the industry to supplement teaching, research projects offered to faculty

- Use of dynamic dashboard
  - A real-time dynamic data base and mapping of capabilities and competencies of faculty and students globally accessible for matching student capabilities with industry requirements and for collective identification of faculty competencies in specific areas of research and consultancy
  - To be exploited in Phase II of TEQIP.

Section Four: Lessons for Other Indian States or Other Countries

- Faculty development and empowerment is vital for institutional development
- Industry interaction is crucial to ensure relevant technical education and bring industry into the campus
- International linkages create visibility and Karnataka today has global footprints
- Networking—formal and non-formal, enhances collective competencies to undertake large-scale research and consultancy
- Dynamic dashboard is a window on the technical competencies and capabilities of Karnataka for the corporate world.

West Bengal[13]

Section One: Context, Size, and Shape of the Higher Education Sector

State Profile:

- Total geographic area: 88,752 square km
- Total population: 80 million (approx)
- Male-female ratio: 52:48
- Percentage of literates: 77 percent (M), 60 percent (F)
- Per capita income: Rs. 28,753

Education Profile 2008–09 (Update 2008)

- School Education
  - Number of schools up to class XII: 71,961
  - Number of students enrolled: 1,77,78,333
  - Male-female ratio: 54: 46

- Technical Education (Polytechnic/ITI level)
  - Number of ITI/ITC: 66
  - Number of Polytechnic (Diploma Colleges): 57
  - Number of Students enrolled: 23,865

- Higher Education
  - State Universities under Higher Education Department: 12
  - State Universities under Other Departments: 6
  - Deemed University (RKMVERI): 1
  - Central Universities: 2
  - Institutes with special status: 5 (IIT–K, IIM–K, ISI, NIT, IISER–K)
  - Institutes of National Importance: 1 (Asiatic Society)
  - Important Research Institutes: 11

- Total Number of Colleges: 751 (Government Colleges only 37)

- Higher Education Budget (2008–09): Rs. 987 crores (US$205.625 million) (2 percent of total State Budget and 12.3 percent of total Education Budget)

- Higher Technical Education

  - State Universities: 6
  - Government Engineering Colleges: 06
  - Self Financing Private Colleges: 60
  - MBA Colleges: 37
  - MCA Colleges: 32
  - Hotel Management Colleges: 4
  - Total number of students enrolled per year in higher education: 24,000 (approx)
  - Total number of faculty: about 5,000

West Bengal has a glorious tradition of education through establishment of Calcutta University in the year 1857, Bengal Engineering College (now BESU) in 1856, and subsequently Jadavpur University in 1955. The Government of West Bengal maintained good standard of technical education since pre independence era. West Bengal University of Technology was established in 2001. No private university exists in the state.

Figure 3.2. Growth of Engineering Institutions in West Bengal

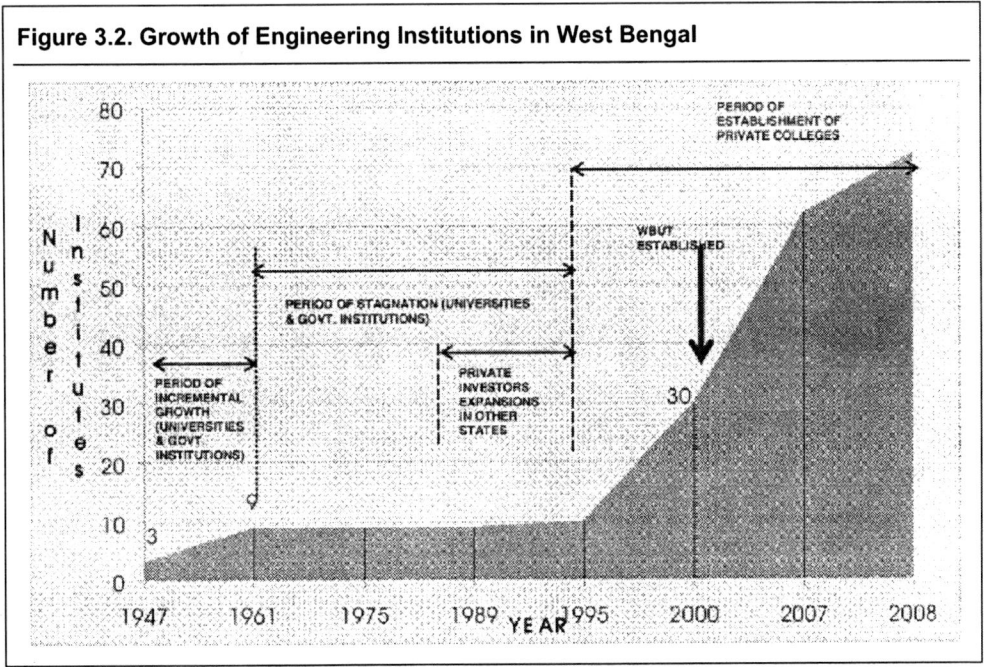

Source: State Government of West Bengal.

Unique Features of the State

- All government and private engineering colleges are under one affiliating university (WBUT)
- All private engineering colleges have the Uniform fee structure as recommended by the Fee Structure Committee
- The State Joint Entrance Exam requires no domicile criteria for admission to any private engineering college in the state

Section Two: Specific Governance Arrangements

Higher Education Policies

- Expansion of access to higher education and decentralization of powerbase
- Equity in educational opportunity and social justice
- Consolidation and qualitative improvement of colleges and expanding the base of social relevance of higher education
- Linkage of education to employment through knowledge and skill upgrading
- Accountability at all levels

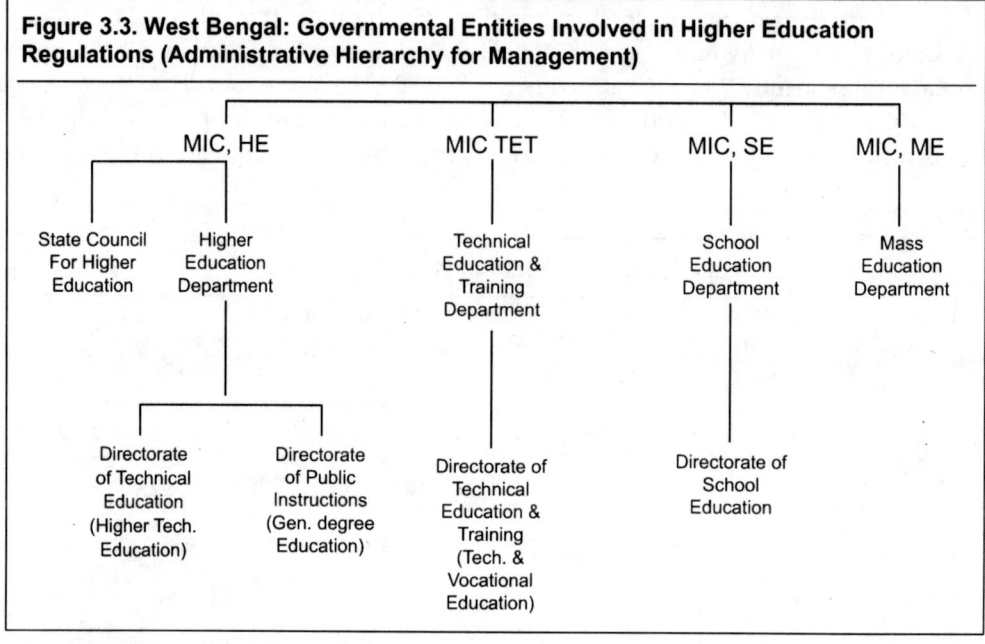

Figure 3.3. West Bengal: Governmental Entities Involved in Higher Education Regulations (Administrative Hierarchy for Management)

Source: State Government of West Bengal.

Section Three and Section Four: Recent Reforms in Higher Technical Education/Lessons for Others

Until the late 1990s higher technical education was primarily confined within a few government-controlled engineering institutions and very old state universities in West Bengal. Conventional teaching and learning with vocationalization of education were the primary focus. Consolidation of education with very little growth was the agenda. The first reformation took place after the late nineties when the state government allowed private participation in the growth of Higher Technical Education. As a result two private self-financing engineering colleges were established first in the year 1996, followed by sporadic exponential growth thereafter.

The second reformation took place when the state government decided to make a significant change in the evaluation process of State Joint Entrance Examination from subjective to objective assessment along with many other tangible modifications since the year 2005–06.

The third reformation was the mandate given by the state government to constitute the governing body in each and every engineering college as per the AICTE guidelines and laid down detail procedures.

The performance of private self-financing colleges is monitored regularly. In order to improve quality of teaching a continuous thrust has been given to apply for NBA accreditation for each college. The state government has activated the BOGs to ensure introduction of at least two core disciplines in each institution.

One of the most remarkable reformation measures is the sincere drives of the private self-financing engineering colleges to institutionalize merit cum means scholarship for academically good but economically poor students in lien admission against management quota.

Significant institutional reforms, both academic and non-academic, were introduced from 2005 to 2009 through implementation of TEQIP. Practice of autonomy with accountability by the institutes has also been ensured.

Academic Reforms

WBUT granted autonomy to the TEQIP institutes to introduce elective subjects at the undergraduate level as per market demand as well as full autonomy to the PG Courses except conducting examination and awarding degree. Evaluation of teachers by students and teacher's counseling; encouraging institutes to develop synergic networking with institutes of repute through sharing of physical and human resources; Granting incentive to the faculty, and staff to conduct continuing education scheme, sponsored research programs, and so forth have been introduced. Qualification and skill up-gradation of faculty and staff has been undertaken as a continuous program.

Non-Academic Reforms

Financial autonomy through block grant funding of non-salary non-plan expenditures with authority to appropriate and re-appropriate; retention of tuition and other fees for ensuring sustainability of the reforms process; authority to generate, retain and utilize internally generated revenue (IRG) through different academic and non academic activities; Establishment of four funds—Corpus, Staff Development, Maintenance and Depreciation Funds—to create financial strength of the institutes to sustain autonomy.

These institutional reforms initially introduced in TEQIP institutions have already been extended to the public funded non-TEQIP institutions.

Institutional reform has become a culture in this state.

Specific Governance Developments

- All recognized engineering institutions in the state are AICTE approved and university affiliated.
- All institutions have their own board of management/governing body, on which stakeholders have representation.
- All institutions are under the strong academic control of the university for quality upgradation.

Notes

[1] By State Government of Andhra Pradesh.

[2] APSCHE came into existence on 20th May, 1988 through an Act (No. 16 of 1988) of the State Legislature.

[3] Source of information for 2008-09 is APSCHE website: www.apsche.org

[4] G.O.P. No. 646, Dated: 10.07.1979 issued by Education (W) Department, Government of Andhra Pradesh.

[5] G.O.Ms. No. 53, 54, and 60 higher education (EC-2) Department Dated: 10.05.2006, 10.05.2006 and 26.05.2006 respectively issued by Government of Andhra Pradesh.

[6] (AFRC) headed by a retired judge constituted as per the Supreme Court Judgment.

[7] As per the data available in NBA website: www.nba-aicte.ernet.in.

[8] APSCHE conducted rationalization of faculty and the state government enabled the Universities to fill the posts accordingly in 2006–07.

[9] G.O.Ms.No. 61 higher education (TE-II) Department dated: 28.06.2005

[10] RGUKT website: www.rgukt.in.
[11] By State Government of Haryana.
[12] By State Government of Karnataka.
[13] By State Government of West Bengal.

CHAPTER 4

National and International Case Studies

Arun Nigavekar
Rong Wang
Tsutomu Kimura
Aims McGuinness
Andrew Cubie
Jannette Cheong

India[1]

Section One: Context, Size, and Shape of the Higher Education Sector

Indian higher and technical education system is huge and complex. India has a federal governmental structure: there is a central government and there are state governments (30 in number). Education is funded both by central and state governments. The Ministry of Human Resource Development (MHRD) at the national level and the Education Ministry in each state decide on policy, its implementation, and give financial support. The University Grants Commission is an apex body that decides national policy on growth and funding for higher education and also monitors standards and makes judgments on quality. In addition, there are Professional Councils set up through an Act of Parliament by the central government.[2] Professional councils are responsible for recognition of courses, promotion of professional institutions and provide support grants to initiate or strengthen undergraduate programs and various awards.

There are different types of universities and they can be grouped as follows:

- Universities/Institutions of National Importance created by Act of Parliament
  - Central Universities
  - Deemed-to-be-Universities (these institutions are recognized as Deemed-to-be-Universities by UGC)
  - Indian Institutes of Technology (IIT)
  - Indian Institutes of Scientific Education, and Research (IISER)
  - Indian Institutes of Management (IIM)

- Universities created by the Act of State Legislature
  - State University
  - Private University

The growth of Indian education has been phenomenal as could be seen in table 4.1

Table 4.1. Growth of Indian Education

Year	Universities*	Colleges	Enrollment (Millions)
1947–48	20	496	0.2
1950–51	28	578	0.28
1960–61	45	1,819	0.60
1970–71	93	3,277	2.0
1980–81	123	4,738	2.8
1990–91	164	5,748	4.4
2000–01	266	11,146	8.8
2007–08	442	18,627	11.5

Source: UGC.
* Includes central, state, deemed-to-be, and private universities and Institutions of National Importance. The data is for both conventional and open universities

Higher education covers post-secondary education (beyond class 12) with four levels of qualifications; Bachelors', Masters', pre-doctoral (M.Phil), and doctoral (Ph.D.) (durations of Bachelors' and Masters' vary with disciplines where as M.Phil. is of 18 months and for Ph.D. minimum work period is two years).

Engineering education became a main attraction after 1990 when India became a major contributor to the global IT industry revolution. Presently, engineering undergraduate degrees specializing in mechanical, electrical, civil, telecommunication, electronics, information technology, computer hardware, and software, are enormously popular with students.

After the 1980s many state governments encouraged the idea of self-financed professional colleges where state government does not provide financial support but facilitates the setting up of such institutions by providing land and other infrastructural support at subsidized rates. This idea was well received by states in Southern and Western parts of India where four states (Tamil Nadu, Karnataka, Andhra Pradesh and Maharashtra) have more than 50 percent of total engineering colleges in India.

The overall participation rate in Indian higher education is 11.7. Professional education is 13 percent of the student (higher education) population.

Section Two: Specific Governance Arrangements

The status of engineering colleges/institutions varies:

■ State universities
- Affiliated college; common curriculum, examination held by the university, degree given by the affiliating university
- Affiliated but autonomous; curriculum decided by the college, examination conducted by the college, degree given by the affiliating university

■ Central Universities
- Constituent College; curriculum decided by the college, examination by the college, degree given by the university

- Deemed-to-be-Universities
  - Constituent College; curriculum decided by the college, examination by the college, degree given by the university

- IITs
  - B. Tech. degree; autonomous departments, curriculum decided by the department, examination by the department, degree given by the Institute.

Governance Structure for Academic Operations Only

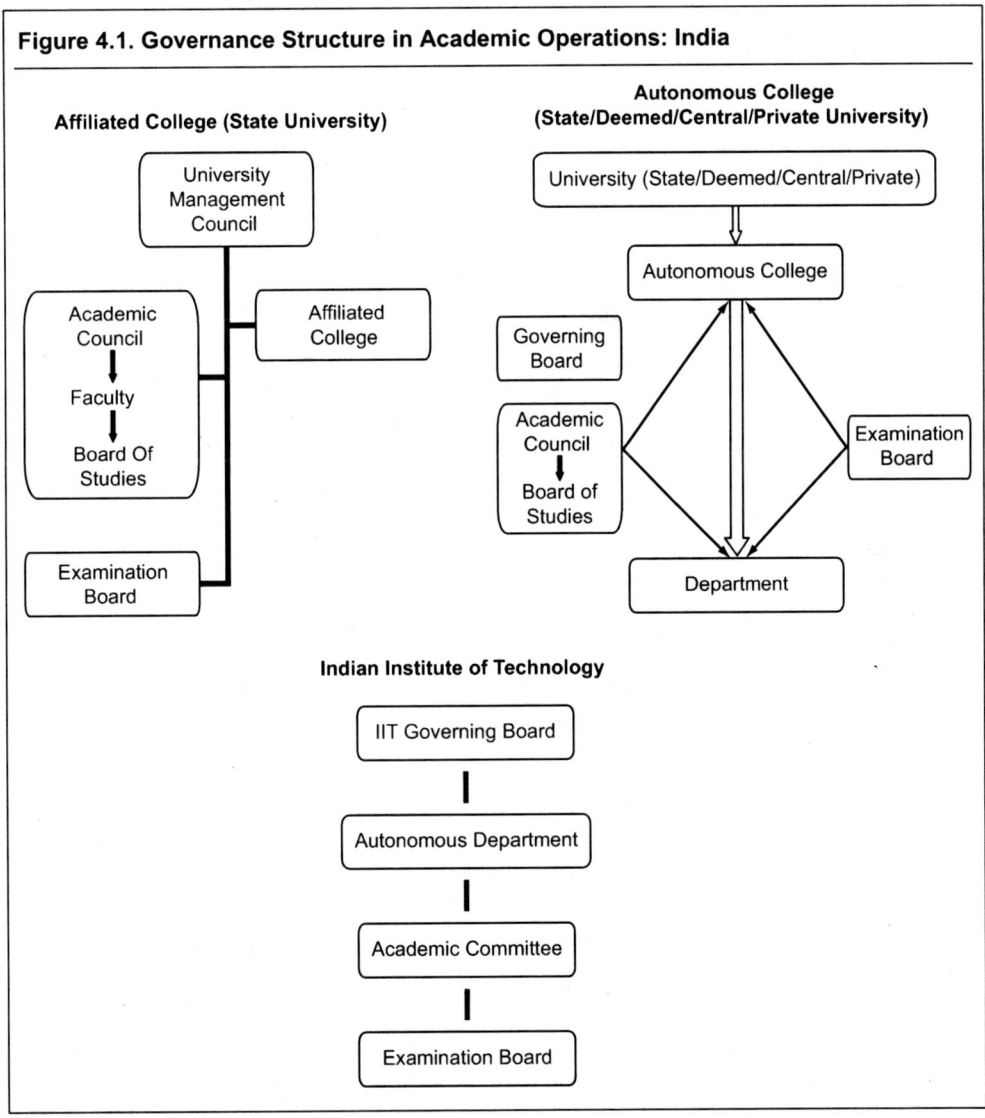

Figure 4.1. Governance Structure in Academic Operations: India

Source: Authors.

Budget

The Indian professional education system over the years has evolved a public, private, and sometimes mixed financial resource generation system. Presented below are the sources of finance for various types of institutions.

State Autonomous and Affiliated Colleges: State government provides the finances for both capital investments and running expenses (salary, maintenance and contingencies). The colleges are encouraged to enhance budgetary support through industrial consultancy and contractual research. The money so earned is retained within colleges. There is variation as regards retention of collected fees. In some states collected fees are taken into account while making the total budgetary provision where as in some states they are taken into account while deciding capital and recurring expenses but the entire salary cost is paid by the state.

Central Universities: The UGC fully supports the capital and running cost. Funds generated through industrial consultancy and research are retained within departments/colleges. The university retains the fee revenue. In addition, UGC gives core development grants under five-year plan and there are many other schemes for supporting academic, research, support and physical infrastructure. The central universities get more generous funds from UGC than state universities.

IITs: The MHRD fully supports the capital and running cost. Indeed the funding to IITs is more generous. Funds generated through industrial consultancy and research is retained with Departments/colleges. The fee revenue is retained by the IITs.

Deemed-To-Be-Universities and State Private Universities: Most deemed universities are self financed and they do not get any support funds, except for research, either from state or central governments. It is because of this the fee structure in these universities is at a much higher level compared to state public universities, IITs, and central universities.

It is mostly input based deficit financing (In annual budget) in state and central universities that nurtures the status quo. The central universities do get larger percentage of grants under the central governments five-year plan compared to state universities. IITs are better off in respect of plan funds and they also generate more funds through consultancy projects and research grants.

Fees

State/central government regulates the fee structure in all the universities/institutions. The fees for state university institutions is decided by the State Fee Committee which takes the audited accounts statement for the previous three years and looks at depleted infrastructure development cost, academic cost (laboratories, equipments, library, IT support services, salaries of teaching and support staff) and also other support services (hostels, sports, medical facilities). It also takes into account the report of accrediting agencies. Thus fees for a given course that is taught in different institutions may vary. Indeed it indicates for parents, albeit indirectly, the quality of teaching in institutions.

It is deemed-to-be-universities, even though they are to follow UGC/MHRD norms, which have very large fees. They also collect additional charges from students for every other support service. There are several aberrations and in spite of many Supreme Court judgments in response to Public Interest Litigations. The absence of a clear unambiguous policy by the central government allows these universities to thrive on an uncontrolled fee structure.

Faculty

The Act, both for central and state universities, does provide clarity in the process of selection of faculty. UGC and AICTE also issue guidelines for minimum qualifications for appointment of Teachers in professional colleges. The selection process is followed by most of the colleges. The salary scales are also announced by the central governments and recent pay scales review is substantial and it is hoped good qualified persons would opt to enter the teaching profession. However, there is an acute shortage of good teachers, hence many self-financed colleges give additional financial advantage or perks to attract to best talent.

Quality

There are two assessment and accreditation agencies, one set up by UGC (the National Assessment and Accreditation Council (NAAC)) and the other by AICTE (the National Board of Accreditation (NBA)). It is now mandatory for colleges/institutions to get their degree programs and institutions assessed by NBA before they launch an activity (NBA accredits professional courses/programs, including engineering). Many institutions/colleges do both NAAC and NBA assessment process (NB: NAAC is an autonomous quality assessment and accreditation body).

Deemed-to-be-universities are expected to go through both NAAC and NBA assessment and accreditation processes. The signing of Washington Accord by AICTE has brought in further critical analysis in accreditation process.

Other

There are several reports published by NASSCOM, CII, and FICCI (Federation of Indian Chambers of Commerce and Industry) that indicate that only 25 percent of engineering graduates are found employable and they also need further in-house training before they are given job assignments. It is felt that poor academic and other support infrastructure and shortage of good faculty and also lack of real time experience during under-graduates study program is a real cause for this state of affairs. There is also a possibility that alternate path for admissions (management quota for each institution/college) bring in non-merit students in the stream thereby affecting the quality of final product.

The educational system faces many challenges and they are mostly linked with policy matters related to governance. Even though economic reforms in last two decades have enhanced the percentage of middle class (estimated at 45 percent) large number of families finds it difficult to meet the high cost of professional education. The government has yet to devise an approach that would maintain a balance between treating higher and technical education as a "merit and non-merit good." This means the ambiguities and differences in fee structure in public and self-financed institutions would continue to haunt families.

Section Three: Recent Reforms That Have Taken Place Related to Governance

There are no laws in respect of this, though UGC and AICTE have issued guidelines in respect of autonomy and accountability of higher education.

Indian higher and technical education system is struggling with reforms (at academic and governance level) for last few decades with partial success. This has happened because of absence of uniform policy that is acceptable to central and state governments. Even though the public in general is aware of the need for relevant and quality education (and also bearing the large cost of education) and is looking for cohesive policy and uniform geographical spread of access at affordable cost, no serious attempts have been done by the central government to bring in order in the education system. The TEQIP activity, which took place between March 2003 and March 2009 and which was mainly funded by the World Bank, has achieved in 127 institutions:

- Promotion of academic excellence
- Networking among institutions to share academic resources
- Enhancement of reach of services to community
- Promoted governance capacity improvement.

However, the challenge is big (TEQIP touched hardly 10 percent of institutions) and serious organized and converging efforts are the need of the day.

The recent reports by the Knowledge Commission and Yash Pal Committee would become a focal point for change as announced by the government elected in 2009.

Section Four: Lessons for Other Countries

Issues being discussed in India:

- Review of monitoring bodies
- Status for proposed Commission for Higher Education and Research?
- Institutional autonomy, and diversity
- Improvement in the management of HEIs and appointment of vice-chancellors
- Broaden single discipline institutions?
- Appropriate public-private partnership
- Focus on inviting leading academics, and scientists (rather than encouraging foreign institutions to set up shop)?

As said earlier, Indian higher and technical education system is huge and complex. It has grown enormously and still struggling with access, excellence, quality, resources, and governance. However, the shear advantage of number (and small fraction of brilliant and innovative students among the two and a half million young minds that are pursuing engineering education) and also few very good institutions/colleges that are imparting education and skills at global standards has given India advantage in accepting challenges in the twenty-first century global economy. The next five years will be crucial and it is hoped that several core level reforms will take place that will enhance the utility and quality of education. There will be converging approaches between accountability and governance with greater autonomy to institutions.

The story of India's struggle and the expected positive outcome would be of immense value for other nations.

China[3]

Section One: Context, Size, and Shape of the Higher Education Sector

Overall Educational Development in China

- The adult illiterate rate: declined to 9.31 percent in 2005 for the population aged 15 and over, 4.87 percent for males and 13.72 percent for females respectively.

- Gross enrollment rate for primary education in 2007 reached 106.2 percent, 98 percent for junior secondary education, and 66 percent for senior secondary education.[4]

- In the mean time, the higher education sector has also undergone enormous change since 1999. Gross enrollment rate in higher education rose from 3.4 percent in 1990 to 9.8 percent in 1998 and to 23 percent in 2007. The number of HEIs increased from 1022 in 1998 to 1908 in 2007, and the total enrollment from 3.4 million to more than 18 million.

There are four types of higher education institutions: post-graduate training institutions, regular HEIs, adult HEIs and non-state/private HEIs. In 2007, there are 795 post-graduate training institutions, of which 479 are regular HEIs and the rest are research institutes independent from regular HEIs. For the 1,908 regular HEIs, in terms of the academic degree hierarchy, 740 of them are the "university" institutions with accreditation to offer bachelor's degree and beyond (in which case they also fall into the category of post-graduate training institutions as discussed in Section Two of this case study), the other 1,168 are the "non-university" institutions offering academic degree below bachelor's degree and most of them, 1,015, are categorized as tertiary vocational and technical college. In 2007 there are 413 adult HEIs and 906 non-state/private HEIs.

Ownership: Public HEIs constitute the majority in China. After the People's Republic of China was founded in 1949, private colleges and universities were eliminated. It is only after the 1980s that private HEIs began to emerge again and gradually consolidated their legal status, with the enactment of Private Education Promotion Law in 2003 as an important policy development milestone. However, elite HEIs remain in the public sector and private ones, though growing very fast, play only a complementary role in China's system.

A defining governance feature for an individual regular public HEI is to which level of government it belongs.

- Of the 1908 regular public HEIs: 111 are central government, (of which 73 are under the direct governance of the Ministry of Education), representing the top tier of the Chinese higher education hierarchy. Except for five HEIs all of the central government institutions are "universities."

- For the 1,502 local authority HEIs: 604 are universities, and 898 are 'non-university' institutions.

There are four levels of HEI degree programs: short-cycle course (zhuan-ke) (2–3 years), bachelor's degree (usually 4 years, but some are 5 years, such as B.M. and engineering), master's degree (2–3 years), and doctoral degree (3 or 4 years).

Scope and size of engineering and technical education in China. There are two relevant indicators.

■   According to the classification of institutions, of the 1908 regular HEIs, 672 are the so-called institutions of natural sciences and technology, which constitutes the largest group.[5] The total enrollment of undergraduate students at such institutions numbered 6,744,874 in 2007, the total enrollment at all regular HEIs is 18,848,954.

■   The second indicator is the distribution of students across fields of study, 6,720,538 students fall into the category of engineering field of study in 2007.[6]

Section Two: Specific Governance Arrangements

Since 1999 China's higher education sector underwent enormous change and the major features of which include:

■   A dramatic switch from the elite tradition to mass higher education
■   Localization of HEIs which used to belong to ministries at the central level
■   Structural streamlining of the regulatory and governance framework, which has resulted in a two-tier system of governance, consisting of the central authority and provincial authorities
■   Mergers of HEIs in the same locality to improve institutional efficiency
■   Adoption of costs-sharing policies and the establishment of multi-channel approach to fund-raising.

The above reforms have had serious impact upon governance arrangements of strategic planning, budgeting and quality assurance of individual HEIs and the whole system.

In 1999 the central government made the policy of expanding higher education dramatically. In tandem with the expansion a series of reforms implemented, including localization. Many institutions belonged to, and were supported by, 'line industry' ministries in the central government in the 'planned economy'. At the end of 1990s efforts to localize such institutions intensified along with the transition of the function of the central government. Many of such institutions were transferred to *provincial government control*; some were ultimately merged with other institutions in the same locality. The number of HEIs of the central government declined from more than 400 in early 1990s to 111 in 2007. Between 1998 and 2006, the number of enrollment at HEIs belonging to the central government increased from 1.15 million to 1.66 million, while the number increased from 2.26 million to 15.73 million for HEIs belonging to local authorities (including independent colleges [du-li-xue-yuan]). This has resulted in local institutions absorbing most of the new intakes in the course of higher education expansion in China.

Differentiation of institutions: As mentioned above, the expansion of educational access has been achieved mainly by opening door wider at non-elite institutions. In the mean time, efforts to build world-class universities intensified. Top universities have been provided additional funding from government under the "985 Project" and "211 Project." The objective of the first one is to support a small group of universities to achieve and sustain a position of "world-class." The "211 Project" scheme has been provided to support a larger number of universities (over 100), to ensure that higher academic standards are maintained.

Another important reform is the adoption of cost-sharing policies. In 1998 China's HEIs collected RMB 7.31 billion in total from student tuition and fees, and the amount rose to 29.8 billion in 2001. The year 2006 saw the figure further jump to RMB 90 billion. During the same period, the share of student tuition and fees in total revenues for regular HEIs climbed from 14.29 percent to 29 percent in 2006.

HEIs in China remain highly bureaucratic from the ownership perspective: government is the owner of public HEIs and holds the ultimate decision-making authority in terms of strategic planning, personnel and budgeting. There is no defined boundary of government intervention into HEIs' affairs and there exists no definite legal and policy backing of counter-intervention of HEIs toward government. From this point of view, the bureaucratic mechanisms are the most important and the most relied-on means of governance towards educational HEIs in China.

A most important institutional arrangement of the Chinese system is the national college entrance exam, which remains to a great extent the single most important criterion Chinese HEIs use to recruit students. This used to be highly centralized, designed by the Ministry of Education with a single set of exam sheets to test all students nationwide. In recent years reforms, intended to localize and introduce more flexibility into the system have been carried out, subjects tested have been reduced, and provinces (municipalities) have been gradually granted partial autonomy. However, the state monopoly over the national entrance exams, that is, the management of admissions to HEIs, helps to sustain the very strong control of the state over educational institutions, including those at both the higher education level and the basic education level, and including those both public and private. By the exams the state de facto regulates the most important input factor of higher education—quality and quantity of students—for every HEI in the sector, thereby ensures the institutional quality.

According to the broader definition of quality assurance mechanisms, there are three major means of regulation of the government over quality matters of HEIs:

- The national college entrance exams, still under the central control to a great extent, are the most important measure of quality control exerted by the government.
- The state exerts control also by appointment of its agents at HEIs. According to Article 39 of China's Higher Education Law, "in HEIs run by the state, the system shall be applied under which the presidents take over-all responsibility under the leadership of the primary committees of the Communist party of China in HEIs."
- In addition, there are a variety of routine quality assurance mechanisms, which constitute the narrowly defined quality assurance system for HEIs in the sector. The major governing bodies at the central level include:
  - The Academic Degrees Committee (ADC) of the State Council. It is responsible for defining different standards for the degrees of B.A., M.A., and Ph.D. The existence of a centralized state degree system is an

important feature of the relationship between HEIs and government in China.

- A Committee for Accreditation, supported by the Educational Development and Planning Division of MOE, defines qualification procedures for assessing relevant educational capacities of an individual HEI in order to grant permission for the establishment of HEI.
- In addition, HEIs are subject to periodic appraisal and evaluations of their academic programs and rights to grant degrees, part of this responsibility lies with the Higher Education Department of Ministry of Education at the central level. An objective of this systematic quality control process is to raise the level of general education provision requirements and to improve the overall quality of HEIs and of the wider schooling system of China.

The most important policy related to student tuition and fees in public HEIs is the "25 percent policy." In the Higher Education Tuition Collection Temporary Regulations issued on December 16, 1996, it is stipulated that for HEIs, "tuition should be determined as a certain percentage of per student educational training costs," furthermore the state made the policy that the percentage of tuition in per student educational training costs should not exceed 25 percent. The central government and provincial governments hold the final decision-making authority over the standards of student tuition and fees and the range of flexibility for institutions under their governance.

Section Three: Recent Reforms That Have Taken Place Related to Governance

At present the most important developing trend in China's higher education system is the increasing prominence of hybrid model of development, which leads to blurred boundary between government and market in educational provision, and complicated nature of ownership of Chinese education institutions. By hybrid, we are referring to several kinds of institutional innovations in China's education sector.

- First, is the hybrid of market and government incentives prevalent at HEIs due to policies of diversifying revenues.
- Second, the existence of "one institution, two systems," meaning some HEIs directly engage in establishing subordinate institutions of private ownership or mixed ownership, for example, independent colleges.

Chronicle of Educational Reform Policies and Legislation in China Since 1980s

- **1984:** The state government decided for HEIs to recruit a certain number of self-financing and enterprise-financing college students.
- **1986:** The state began to adopt more flexible policies in accepting social donations from overseas for colleges and universities.
- **1988:** The government began to implement the policy of "making fixed amount of budget to colleges and universities, allowing residuals be retained," which started to endow institutions more autonomy and encourage the latter's self-initiatives.
- **1989:** Experiments of charging student tuition were carried out in a few colleges and the tuition was set at RMB 100. Despite the very low standard, it indicated the dawning of a new era in college financing.

■ **1991**: The then State Education Commission issued Education Inspection Temporary Regulations, which is the first legal document related to education inspection after the Culture Revolution.

■ **1993**: The central government issued Guidelines on Reform and Development of Chinese Education, in which it is advocated that the state shall institute a system of educational finance in which fiscal allocations constitute the main source, to be supplemented by funds through a variety of avenues.

■ **1994**: Pilots were carried out in 37 colleges and universities to reform the dual track system of recruitment and tuition, that is, self-financing students and state-financing students. By 1997, the reform was completed and all college entrants were required to pay tuition, which was gradually modified and set at 25 percent of educational training costs per student.

■ **1998**: Higher Education Law was enacted, in which the policy of diversification of educational revenues was included.

■ **1999**: Pilots of state student loans programs were carried out in eight cities nationwide. In 2001 the State Student Loans Program Coordination Group was set up with participation of China People's Bank, Ministry of Finance, and Ministry of Education.

■ **1999**: The state began to implement the World Class University Development Plan, in particular provided 1.8 billion respectively to Peking University and Tsinghua University over the period of three years and some other top institutions with less yet substantial support. Implementation of the plan stimulated internal institutional reforms.

■ **2003**: Private Education Promotion Law was enacted.

Table 4.2. A Summary of Major Articles in the Educational Laws Related to Finance, Provision, and Quality Assurance in China's HEIs

The Education Law (1995)	
Finance	• (Article 25) No organization or individual may operate a school or any other type of educational institution for profit
	• (Article 53) The State shall institute a system of educational finance in which fiscal allocations constitute the main source, to be supplemented by funds raised through a variety of avenues in an effort to gradually increase the input of financial resources directed to education so as to ensure that state-run educational institutions have stable sources of funding
	• (Article 53) For a school or an institution of another type sponsored and run by an enterprise or institution or a non-governmental organization or other social body or individual(s)...the people's governments at various levels may provide suitable financial support.
	• (Article 54) The State shall gradually raise the proportion of educational expenditure in gross national product...
	• (Article 55) The educational expenditure of the people's governments at various levels shall be listed separately in their respective fiscal budgets, according to the principle of the unification of the powers of office and the power over financial affairs
Provision	• (Article14):The State Council and local people's governments at all levels shall guide and administer educational work according to the principles of management at different levels with suitable division of responsibility
	• (Article 25) The State shall encourage enterprises, institutions, public organizations, other social groups as well as individual citizens to operate schools or other types of educational institutions in accordance with the law

Quality Assurance	• (Article 20). The State shall institute a national education examination system
	• (Article 21) The State shall institute a system of education certificates.
	• (Article 22) The State shall institute a system of academic degrees
	• (Article 24) The State shall institute an educational inspection system and an educational evaluation system for schools and other types of educational institutions

Regulations of the People's Republic of China on Academic Degrees

Quality Assurance	• (Article 7) The State Council shall establish an Academic Degrees Committee to direct the work of conferring academic degrees throughout the country
	• (Article 8) The bachelors' degree shall be conferred by those institutions of higher learning authorized by the State Council. The master's and doctor's degrees shall be conferred by those institutions of higher learning and scientific research institutions authorized by the State Council
	• A list of institutions of higher learning and scientific institutes that may confer academic degrees and the disciplines in which academic degrees may be conferred shall be submitted to the State Council by its Academic Degrees Committee for approval and promulgation

The Higher Education Law (1999)

Provision	• (Article 6) The State encourages all sectors of society, including enterprises, institutions, public organizations or groups as well as individual citizens, to run HEIs...
	• (Article 29) The establishment of HEIs shall be subject to examination and approval by the administrative department for education under the State Council, the ones for special course education may be subject to examination and approval by the people's government of provinces, autonomous regions and municipalities directly under the central government that are authorized by the State Council.
	• (Article 33) Higher education institutions shall,...,acting on their own in offering and readjusting the branches of learning and specialized subjects.
	• (Article 34) Higher education institutions shall,......acting on their own in drawing up their teaching programs...
	• (Article 35) Higher education institutions shall, ...acting on their own in conducting research, developing technology and providing services for the society.

Source: *The Laws on Education of the People's Republic of China,* compiled by the Ministry of Education of the People's Republic of China, Foreign Language Press, Beijing, 1999. http://www.moe. edu.cn/jyfg/laws/ mbjycjf.htm.

Section Four: Lessons for Other Countries

There are ongoing reforms of higher education in China. It is difficult to know what other countries might learn from China at this time, but as we continue to reform our higher education system there are lessons we ourselves are learning and we are willing to share these with other countries, and equally to learn from them.

Japan[7]

Section One: Context, Size, and Shape[8] of the Higher Education Sector

Overview of Japanese Higher Education System

- 86 National Universities: total full-time student enrollment of 624,000
- 589 Private Universities: total full-time student enrollment equals 2,080,000
- 90 Public Prefecture Universities: total full-time student enrollment equals 132,000

The total number of students at Japanese universities is 2,836,000 with 2,521,000 at undergraduate courses, 165,000 at master courses, 74,000 at Ph.D. courses and 76,000 at professional courses. Social science has the largest share of 36 percent and engineering has 16 percent. The number of part-time undergraduate students in Japan is extremely small. The number of part-time graduate students is relatively high (part-time adult students number 53,000 out of a total 260,000—approximately 20 percent). The majority of the part-time students are not self-supported but supported by companies for whom they work.

There are three tiers of technical and engineering education (Tiers 1 and 2 deliver higher education provision):

- 4-Year Universities (765 institutions in total. See above listing for student numbers). Age range: 18–22
- 5-Year Colleges of Technology (64 in total—55 National, 6 Public Prefecture, 3 Private). Age range: 15–20. Total number of students approximately 60,000
- Technical, and Engineering High Schools. Age range: 12-15. Total of 5,500 high schools, 8 percent of which are for technical and engineering subjects.

Higher education participation ratio for Japan is 52 percent and completion ratio is 92 percent.

In 1998 the University Council identified the roles and functions of universities as follows:

- Pursuing world-class research and education
- Training highly-skilled professionals
- Training wide-ranging-professionals
- Carrying high-quality general education
- Carrying out education and research in specific areas (sports, arts and so forth.)
- Carrying out life-long learning for community
- Contribution to society (service to society).

The Council said that each institution is free to choose one or more any of these functions. MEXT (the Ministry of Education, Culture Sports, Science and Technology) policies following this report are targeted at acceleration of differentiation of roles and functions of each institution.

An accreditation type evaluation system was introduced in 2004. All universities in Japan have to receive this evaluation once in seven years. Three evaluation agencies are responsible for carrying out this evaluation. These agencies were authorized by MEXT with their capabilities checked by the Central Council for Education. The evaluation covers the assessment of (mainly) teaching quality. The results of this accreditation type evaluation do not affect funding except for the cases where there is illegal conduct. Each university is free to choose any of these three evaluation agencies.

In addition to these evaluations, all national universities have to receive comprehensive evaluation once in 6 years by an evaluation committee organized by MEXT. The National Institution for Academic Degrees and University Evaluation (NIAD-UE) carries out the evaluation of teaching and research. This scheme was introduced in 2004 following incorporation of national universities. Evaluation results affect 8–9 percent of each university's block grant allocation. The impact of this varies from institution to institution—smaller universities with less alternative funding streams will be affected more than universities with more diversified funding sources.

As a result of the reduction in the younger age population, 40–50 private universities are facing serious economic problems at present. They may go bankrupt. In such cases, the priority will be to protect existing students by transferring them to other universities to ensure minimal disruption to their studies.

Section Two: Specific Governance Arrangements

National Universities

Legal status: National University Corporation

Budget:

- *Block grant allocation:* Block grant allocation is controlled by MEXT in terms of the total amount of money allocated, but universities can decide how they use the money. Tuition fee levels are strictly controlled by MEXT.
- *Capital grant allocation:* Each year applications go through a two-stage process; assessed initially by MEXT and then the Ministry of Finance.

Human resources: Responsibility for contracting, hiring and firing, and salary levels of teaching staff and other administrative and technical staff rests with universities.

- Each university can decide the total number of teaching staff. The same applies to staff training, development plans and funding levels.

Quality assurance system:

- External: External evaluation system was described in Section One.
- The Internal QA system is now closely linked with the external system as a result of the introduction of the new national QA system; evaluation system. All universities are required to submit a self-evaluation report, when they receive accreditation type evaluation. The evaluation committee checks if a university has a 'healthy' '*Plan, do, check*, and *action*' cycle. As a result of this procedure, all national universities now have their own internal evaluation systems.

The governance system is shown in figure 4.2.

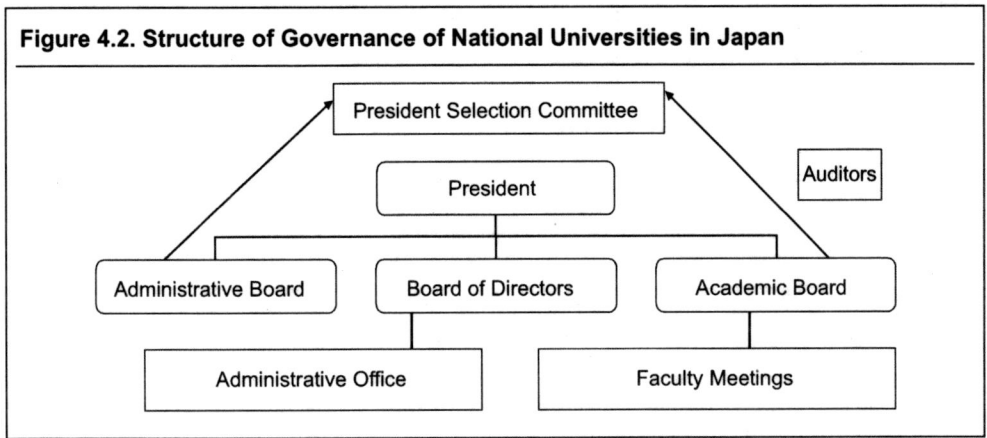

Figure 4.2. Structure of Governance of National Universities in Japan

Source: Author.

This system was introduced when all national universities were incorporated in 2004. The background for this system change will be described in Section Four.

Strategic planning: Strategic plans are decided by MEXT on the whole, but, in recent years, MEXT only shows the general framework of its strategic plans so that each university can decide their own strategic plans within the framework. The Ministry used to produce very detailed strategic plans that tightly controlled the actions of each university.

Private Universities

Legal status: School Corporation

Governance system: Very similar to that for national universities.

Strategic planning: Same as for national universities.

Budget:
The total amount of public funding provided to private universities is approximately 300,000,000,000 yen (approximately US$3 billion). MEXT examines private universities' requests for funding each year and makes an allocation. This part of funding covers mainly the fundamental costs for running a university such as building classrooms for students and offices for staff, and space for research facilities. Private universities can apply for special research grants given by MEXT and other ministries on an equal basis to national universities. Some private universities do not receive any funding from MEXT. The number is very few.

Private university funding relies heavily on tuition fees. Tuition fee levels vary considerably. Final fee levels must be approved by MEXT. Generally speaking, the rate of private university tuition compared to national universities is 1:3 for social sciences and 1:4 for engineering, and for medicine 1:15–20.

Human resources:
Very similar to national universities. But for national universities, the block grant that covers salary for staff is decided by MEXT, and for private universities main source for

staff salary is tuition fee. In that sense, the control by MEXT for private universities is weaker than for national universities.

Quality assurance system:
Exactly same as for national universities for accreditation type evaluation. They now have similar internal QA system to that of national universities.

Public Prefecture Universities

Legal status: Either university corporation or one of the organizations run by local government such as highway corporation or housing corporation.

Governance system: For university corporations the system is very similar to that of national universities. For organizations under local government, the senate consisting of president, deans, members elected by professorial meeting, makes decision on important issues.

Strategic planning: The local government decides strategic plans within the framework put forward by MEXT. This type of Public Prefecture University has less freedom and autonomy than national universities.

Budget and human resources: The responsibility rests with local governments. They receive nearly all their public funding from local governments. They can also apply for special research grant on an equal basis to national and private universities.

Quality assurance system:
- *External:* They have to receive accreditation type evaluation once in seven years as national and private universities.
- *Internal:* As a result, they have developed very similar internal QA systems to national and private universities.

National Colleges of Technology

In engineering, Colleges of Technology, particularly National Colleges of Technology, are now considered extremely important in keeping Japan as one of the strongest countries in manufacturing in the world.

In 2004, 54 National Colleges of Technology were made into one College of Technology corporation, which has a similar governance structure to that of National University Corporation. Each college, however, is allowed to have very limited autonomy. Important decisions are made solely by a principal - the top figure among teaching staff. According to School Educational Law, their obligation is only teaching. As the result of this mechanism, their teaching quality is very high, for which they received high appreciation by OECD higher education reviewers in the report published in 2007. The total number of students they have is 60,000. The graduates from Colleges of Technology are extremely well received by industry. Several years ago when university graduates faced the difficulty of finding employment, graduates from Colleges of Technology enjoyed the situation that even the lowest rate of job offer was 8 per graduate.

Section Three: Recent Reforms That Have Taken Place Related to Governance

Incorporation of national universities took place in 2004. The detail of the reform will be described in Section Four.

Section Four: Lessons for Other Countries

Incorporation of National Universities

In 1998, University Council organized by MEXT published an important report suggesting the future of higher education in Japan, under the title "Creating universities with marked individual characteristics in competitive environments." In that report, the Council said that national universities in Japan would not be able to achieve this goal under the current system and that a new system should be introduced to make them move forward. This led to long discussions in different sectors on the change of the status of national universities. The discussions concluded in 2003 that corporation status should be given to national universities.

Main elements of the system change:

- Deregulation of management through incorporation
- Concentration of authority in the University President
- Target-based indirect control by government: Each university has to describe targets for a mid-term period (six years). Evaluation Committee at MEXT checks if those targets have been achieved. MEXT decides the block grant based on the performance of each university.

The extent of freedom obtained by national universities:

Finance:

- Introduction of block-grant (formula based + item-based)
  - Some budget controls remain: As described above under the heading of "Main elements of the system change"
  - Internal and external Audits strengthened
- Separate funding for Capital Grants
- Tuition fees fixed with some allowance in differentiation: So far no national universities have used this allowance. The tuition fees are same for all national universities.
- Freedom in earning and using non-governmental resources.

Staffing:

- Change of legal status of staff to non-governmental employee
  - Freedom from government's regulation
  - Legal guarantee of faculty's and senate's authority in academic personnel matters repealed.

Organization:

- Establishment and dissolution of fundamental academic units such as departments, post-graduate schools and research institutes stipulated in mid-term plan
- Number of students places in fundamental academic units stipulated in mid-term plan.

Main features of governance:
- Minister of MEXT appoints auditor
- President appoints all university staff except auditors
- Only president can legally represent universities and corporations
- Minister of MEXT appoints and discharges presidents based on the decision of the university's president selection committee (see Section One)
- Inclusion of outside persons is required for auditors, directors and administrative board members.

Main features of target-based control:
- Target-setting based on university's draft: MEXT shows only rough guidelines and checks if the targets are reasonable.
- Target and plan are comprehensive in nature: It is not necessary for each university to set detailed targets and plans for mid-term period. These general targets are broken into detailed yearly plans. Since Evaluation Committee at MEXT assesses the performance of each university once in six years on the basis of mid-term target and plan set by each university, it is rather difficult to assess their performance properly.
- Evaluation by MEXT's National University Evaluation Committee
- Evaluation of teaching and research entrusted to National Institution for Academic Degrees and University Evaluation (NIAD-UE)
- Results of evaluation affect funding.

Impact of Incorporation
- Reduction in block grant expenditure: 1.2415 trillion yen (2004) to 1.1695 trillion yen (2009)
- Steady progress in efficient operations
- Reduction in operational cost: 1.6139 trillion yen (2004) to 1.4084 trillion yen (2007)
- Strategic resource allocation under the initiative of president: funding (at all 86 universities), decision of number of staff and their salary at president's own discretion (at 82 universities). This includes the introduction of special salary for inviting researchers with high profile and tuition waver for students with extremely high performance
- Promotion of fixed term employment system for academic staff: 516 (2000 before incorporation) to 8,816 (2006 at 81 universities)
- Attempts to enhance quality of teaching and to participate in life-long learning community: introduction of strict marking system (GPA) 7 percent (2000) to 48 percent (2006); evaluation of teaching performance of academic staff 28 percent (2000) to 79 percent (2006); number of adult students at graduate courses 4,641 (2000) to 8,067 (2006)
- Introduction of funds from external sources: donation 49.2 billion yen (2000) to 77.6 billion yen (2007); long-term loan from banks (at five universities for construction of veterinary hospital, student dorms international house and so on)

- Active promotion of university-industry links: joint research 11.2 billion yen (2001) to 33.1 billion yen (2007); commissioned research 35.1 billion yen (2001) to 127.9 billion yen (2007); patent application 2001 to 2007 2.4 times, patent loyalty 2001 to 2007 3.2 times; foundation of start-up company 2001 to 2007 3.2 times.

The Republic of Korea[9]

Section One: Context, Size, and Shape of the Higher Education Sector

As of April 1, 2008, Korean higher education included:

- 405 institutions enrolling 3.6 million students (lifelong learning institutions enrolling 300,000 students),
- More than 2,000 education and training institutions overall.

The two largest institutional categories are universities (41 percent) and junior colleges (offering two- and three-year programs) (38 percent).

A key dimension of Korean higher education is the high reliance on the private sector and financing from students and parents through tuition fees to accommodate enrollment growth. Private institutions constitute 84.5 percent of the universities and enroll 78.4 percent of the university-level students. Private junior colleges constitute 90.5 percent of the junior colleges and enroll 95.7 percent of the students at that level. Although private institutions have private founders, they must operate within the framework of the Higher Education Act, the Private School Act, and regulations of the Ministry of Education and Science and other ministries.

National universities and public universities (within the jurisdiction of local governments) constitute only 15 percent of universities and enroll only 22 percent of university students.

Public junior colleges constitute only 9.5 percent of institutions at this level and enroll only 4.3 percent of the students.

Table 4.3. Percentages of Institutions and Students by Institutional Ownership in Korea

Institutional Categories	Percentages by Institutional Ownership			
	National/Public		Private	
	Percent Institutions	Percent Students	Percent Institutions	Percent Students
Universities	15.2	21.6	84.8	78.4
Junior colleges	9.5	4.3	90.5	95.7

Source: OECD Tertiary Review Country Background Report (TRCBR), pp. 12–14.

Korea has experienced an extraordinary increase in HEIs and enrollments over the past quarter century. From 1990 to 2004, the number of institutions increased 58 percent and student enrollments by 110 percent. Significant increases in secondary education completion as well as higher education participation drove higher education-level increases. Liberalization of laws related to the establishment of universities in 1995, led to a surge in establishment of new institutions.

Section Two: Specific Governance Arrangements

Oversight entities

The principal oversight entity for higher education is the Ministry of Education, Science and Technology (MEST). This Ministry consolidates two previously separate ministries, the Ministry of Education and Human Resource Development and the Ministry of Science and Technology. Several other ministries also play significant roles in higher education oversight, as illustrated in table 4.4.

Table 4.4. Governmental Entities involved in Higher Education Regulations

Institution	Main Regulations
Ministry of Education, Science and Technology	Regulations related to school operations such as establishment, student affairs, personnel and financing Regulations regarding the method and results of research related to science and technology
Ministry of Planning, and Budget	Regulations related to the budget allocation and execution of national universities
Ministry of Government Administration and Home Affairs	Regulations regarding the limit on administrative staff for national and public universities
Ministry of Commerce, Industry and Energy	Regulations regarding the execution of industry-academia research and projects
The Korean Intellectual Property Office	Regulations related to the patent application of academic research results
Ministry of Labour	Regulations related to the working conditions and labor practices of private university workers
Ministry of Environment	Regulations related to the disposal of pollutants such as waste at universities and regulations related to the environmental impact analysis
Ministry of Justice	Regulations related to the immigration policies and visa issuance of foreign students
Ministry of Health, and Welfare	Regulations regarding the limits on enrollment in health and medical studies
Ministry of Construction, and Transportation	Regulations related to the establishment of universities in the capital region

Source: OECD Review of Country response, Table 6, p. 32.

From a legal perspective, Korean HEIs (national, public and private) have significant autonomy on academic and substantive issues. Nevertheless, this autonomy is limited in several specific ways that, from the perspective of higher education, restrict essential elements of autonomy:

▓ The Constitution of the Republic of Korea, Article 31, Paragraph 6, requires that the basic rules regarding operation, financing, and the status of teaching staff for education systems, including school and lifelong learning, must be stipulated by law. Therefore, the Higher Education Act and related enforcement decrees regulate activities such as the establishment of universities, organization, curriculum, student selection, and staffing.

▓ Regulations differ according to type and characteristics of the institution (for example, universities, junior colleges, industrial universities, open universities, and so forth.) and founders (the national government, local autonomous governments, or private corporations/education foundations).[10] Regulations areas such as:

• Enrollment quotas, especially as they affect the national budget and limit expansion of enrollments in the Metropolitan Seoul area

• Student selection criteria designed to curb private tutoring driven by the intense competition of students on examinations used for university entrance

- Appointment of academic staff. The Ministry of Education, Science and Technology administers and supervises the appointment of secretary generals, directors and deputy directors at national universities) and controls the appointment of staff at national universities while autonomous local governments have the same responsibilities with respect to public universities
- Budget and financial management. National and public universities have limited autonomy on procedural matters such as budgeting, financial management, purchasing and entering into contracts
- Private institutions have substantial autonomy in the appointment of academic and non-academic staff and on budget and financial management procedural matters such as budgeting, financial management, purchasing and entering into contracts.[11] Nevertheless, private universities are subject to regulations regarding student selection criteria, enrollment quotas in the Seoul Metropolitan area, and composition of governing bodies.[12]

Section Three: Recent Reforms That Have Taken Place Related to Governance

Since the early 1990s, higher education reform in Korea has been central element of the government's strategy to increase the country's competitiveness in the global knowledge-based economy. The concern is that Korea must have a higher quality, more diversified, flexible and responsive higher education system to meet the future needs of the nation.

Major issues driving reform include the following concerns:

- Severe competition to get into prestigious universities is having a negative impact on the quality of secondary education and is a threat to social cohesion.
- Higher education is not prepared for demographic changes: an ageing population, a projected population shortage in the working age population by 2020, and a shrinking college-age population, and continued population concentration in the Seoul Metropolitan area.
- Brain-drain resulting from Korean students increasingly going to foreign universities and Korean universities not attracting foreign students or professors.
- Hierarchical market competition has not led to differentiation but to a "monotonous system," with many universities offering the same profile of academic programs.
- Business and industry leaders are dissatisfied with the knowledge and skills of graduates.

The Korean government has traditionally maintained a tight control over both public and private university operations. Until the early 1990s, almost all aspects of university operations, including the private sector, almost all aspects of university operations were subject to detailed government regulations.

In 1995 there was a major shift in regulatory policy. One of the basic reform principals of the Government of Korea was the full development of school autonomy and reduction of government regulation. Despite consistent emphasis of several governments on increasing autonomy for national and public universities, the government still maintained a high degree of control of most areas of institutional management including personnel, organization, and capital financing.[13]

Since the mid-1990s, increasing university autonomy has been a recurring theme in successive governments' priorities. In 2006, the Governor was seeing support for a "Special Law on National University Administration that would have permitted national Universities to become "school corporations" independent of the formal governmental structure, but the National Assembly did not enact the proposal.

The current government of Korea (assuming office in early 2008), has set forth three broad higher education tasks:

- To reinforce the educational capacity of HEIs
- To pursue a core strategy to raise the autonomy and accountability of HEIs
- Raising the research capacity of HEIs (especially those governing university admissions.

The reforms related to autonomy and accountability are intended to eliminate a major part of regulations imposed on institutions. The reforms include a new approach to university admissions (to counter the impact of the current excessive focus on entrance examinations), new requirements for information disclosure, and a new evaluation and accreditation system. In return, institutions are being required to strengthen accountability and build infrastructure for self-development.[14]

Increasing institutional autonomy remains a government priority, but documents reveal less emphasis than in previous governments on major reforms such as changing the legal status of national universities to "school corporations." The emphasis appears to have shifted to pragmatic, incremental changes that can be implemented within the current political and economic context.

Section Four: Lessons for Other Countries[15]

The following summarizes key lessons from the Korean experience for other countries' reform initiatives:

- "Top-down" implementation of reforms that do not engage faculty and institutional leadership can lead to "paper-based performance and accountability rather than any substantial, enduring change in the education process."
- Academic staff opposition to changes in internal governance (for example, change from election of presidents to presidents as strong executive leaders and external accountability) reflected skepticism grounded in recollections of the authoritarian policies of previous governments.
- Senior professors are often reluctant to relinquish their authority to a stronger executive approach to university leadership or to support increased autonomy because it might jeopardize their special status in a country's laws and traditions, and their dominant role in university collegial self-governance.
- Intractable opposition to reform of long-standing, controversial regulatory policies such as those related to university entrance/admissions policies and enrollment quotes can block attention to more fundamental reforms such as changing the legal status of the national universities.

- It is important to sustain the focus on the basic goals of reform over changes in governments and economic conditions. While the details of reform proposals may differ, successive governments can maintain the commitment to and momentum toward the same underlying long-term goals.
- Sweeping, large-scale reform is often neither desirable nor politically feasible. Failing to achieve broad political support from internal and external stakeholders for massive reform proposals, governments must then pursue step-by-step, incremental changes. This means a change "top-down" massive reform to a more systematic and sustained efforts to build support for fundamental change among internal and external stakeholders.

References

BYUN, Kiyong. "New Public Management in Korean Higher Education: Is It a Reality or Another Fad?" *Asia-Pacific Education Review*, April 2008.

Organisation for Economic Co-operation and Development (OECD). *OECD (2007), OECD Reviews of Regulatory Reform, Korea: Progress in Implementing Regulatory Reform.* Paris: OECD, 2007.

Republic of Korea. *Background Document for OECD Review of Regulation in Korea.* Background report, Seoul: Republic of Korea, 2006.

Republic of Korea. *Background Report for OECD Review of Tertiary Education in Korea.* Background document, Seoul: Republic of Korea, 2006.

Republic of Korea, Ministry of Education, Science and Technology. *Major Policies to Enhance the Competitive Strength of Korean Higher Education.* Policy document, Seoul: Republic of Korea, 2009.

European Trends in Governance in Higher Education[16]

This section will briefly describe trends in governance in higher education in Europe. Europe in this context is not described as made up of countries in membership of the European Union, but those voluntarily involved in the Bologna process. The Bologna process was launched in 1999 by the Ministers of Education and university leaders of 29 countries with a view to creating a European Higher Education Area (EHEA) by 2010. There are now 46 participating countries. The process is supported by the European Commission and the Council of Europe.

The Bologna Process is to provide tools to connect educational systems, not to harmonize such systems. The reforms are based on 10 objectives, the most important of which where agreement has so far been reached relates to a comparable three-cycle degree system for undergraduates (Bachelor degrees) and graduates (Master and PH.D degrees).

At Ministerial meetings held every two years since 2001 Declarations have been made. In the Lisbon Declaration issued in 2007 governments were called upon to give European universities autonomy to allow the implementation of reforms. This stemmed from the recognition that a higher degree of institutional autonomy would improve governance and strengthen leadership at all levels.

The challenge to create, in terms of the Bologna Process, an EHEA by 2010 remains significant, not least to address aspects of greater autonomy for institutions. Many European countries have a tradition of state control and direction of their universities, which sits uneasily with greater autonomy. Likewise, many have followed the Humboldt model of staff and students having key roles in the appointment of Rectors and other senior staff, which is alien to an empowered governing body. Whilst this is not now the position of the United Kingdom, the circumstances of Oxford and Cambridge continue to owe much to the Humboldtian tradition.

In addressing these issues the European Universities Association (EUA), which represents 800 HEIs in each of the participating Bologna countries, called for a further range of reforms in 2007 in the aftermath of the Lisbon Declaration. These related to autonomy and funding and were as follows:-

- "Autonomy: governments are urged to endorse the principle of institutional autonomy so as to accommodate diverse institutional missions and to include
  - Academic autonomy (curricula, programs and research)
  - Financial autonomy (lump sum budgeting)
  - Organizational autonomy (the structure of the university)
  - Staffing autonomy (responsibility for recruitment, salaries and promotion).
- Autonomy should be founded on adequate public funding and should also facilitate the strategic management of public and private income and endowments (from philanthropists, companies, alumni and students) by the universities themselves.
- Governments are urged to benchmark progress against target levels set in relation to both autonomy and funding of universities.
- Universities will strive to reinforce further leadership and strengthen professional management.

Increasing and Diversifying Funding Streams

The EUA continues to be committed to identifying supplementary revenue streams for universities and to promoting modes of governance that support optimal transparency in financial management.

The data collected by the EUA funding working group demonstrate the huge diversity of public funding mechanisms to be found across Europe. They vary enormously in volume, legal base, methodology, policy thrust, and in the degree to which central authorities control institutional budgets.

The EUA will continue its investigations to the point at which it can reliably profile European universities on the basis of an agreed template and elaborate a general costing methodology. This requires more comprehensive mapping of current public funding models, of their legal and financial environments, and of the supplementary income streams available; it therefore touches directly on key features of both the Bologna Process, such as *the social dimension* (access, equity in student support, and affordability), *the international dimension* (attractiveness and competitiveness) *and mobility* (the portability of student support), and the Lisbon Strategy.

The EUA supports the European Commission's goal of increasing investment in higher education to at least 2 percent of GDP within a decade and urges all partners to work together to ensure that this target is met."

As part of the Leuven Louvain-la-Neuve Declaration made in April 2009 Ministers noted "The necessary ongoing reform of higher education systems and policies will continue to be firmly embedded in the European values of institutional autonomy, academic freedom and social equity and will require full participation of students and staff." They subsequently recorded that institutions had gained greater autonomy along with rapidly growing expectations to be responsive to societal needs and in consequence to be accountable.

It will be evident that the trend in the 46 Bologna Process countries is towards greater autonomy. Inevitably, however, rates of progress vary significantly across the continent although there is no wide resistance to the direction of travel. In the speed of that travel, France and the United Kingdom are probably at opposite ends of a spectrum with opposition to institutional change proposed by President Sarkozy remaining significant.

For further information about EUA see http://www.eua.be.

United Kingdom[17]

Section One: Context, Size, and Shape of the Higher Education Sector

Overview of UK Higher Education System

- 169 Higher Education Institutions
- 109 Universities (included in the 169)
- 2,362,815 Students
- 169,995 Academic staff
- £21.0BN Expenditure.

All UK institutions are state funded through three Funding Councils, which are separately established for England, Scotland, and Wales. There is only one private university, the University of Buckingham. The extent to which individual universities receive Funding Council support varies significantly from almost total to less than 25 percent, with the balance of funding arising from a wide variety of sources.

With total income of £21.3BN and expenditure of £21.0BN, the sector currently remains in balance. The mean average income for institution is £110.0M and the mean average student number per institution is 12.245. Eleven institutions have less than £10M of income and 45 greater than £150M. Likewise, the spread of student numbers stretches from 21 with less than 1,000 students and 45 with more than 20,000. The UK spends 0.8 percent as a percentage of GDP (2004) against an OECD average of 1.0 contrasting with the United States of America at 1.0 and Japan at 0.5.

Of the 2,362,815 students their composition is as follows:

Table 4.5. Attendance in UK Higher Education

All students	Full time	Part time	All
UK	1,189,390	821,955	2,011,345
Other EU	81,335	30,925	112,260
Non EU	180,990	58,220	239,210
Total	1,451,715	911,100	2,362,815

Source: Author based upon data from Higher Education Statistics Agency.

Included in the total figure of 2,362,815 are 559,390 postgraduate students of whom 48,025 are from other EU countries and 136,220 are from non-EU.

These students are taught by 169,995 academic staff, of whom 42 percent are female, 26 percent are under 35 years of age and 20 percent are over 55. However, of professorial appointments only 18 percent are female of any age.

Participation rates vary across England, Scotland, Wales and Northern Ireland, but the average is currently taken as 46 percent, although the cohort groups across those countries is not entirely consistent.

It is hard to break out accurately those institutions offering technical and engineering provision, but a best estimate would be some 75 percent. Whilst all will sustain a teaching provision, not all will undertake research of significance. (Note all figures are taken for 2006/07 unless indicated otherwise.)

For further information about the UK higher education system see: www.universitiesuk.ac.uk; www.hesa.ac.uk.

Section Two: Specific Governance Arrangements

In the current year as a result of the current economic state applications for admission to HEIs have increased dramatically. Whilst no institution is known to be in acute financial distress governing bodies are engaged in a range of cost-reduction measures ranging from reorganization, collaboration, redundancy and capital expenditure deferral.

For centuries in the UK HEIs have been regarded as having not-for-profit status, and that continues today for all UK institutions. This means that each institution must comply with the requirements of charity law as it applies across the UK. Whilst this is broadly the same in its application, there are some variations across England, Northern Ireland, Scotland and Wales. However, each institution requires by law to have a group of Trustees, or governing body, which has legal liability for the good governance of the institution. Such governing body has overall responsibility for the strategic direction, vision, mission, governance and delivery of the institution. Of course, in practice many aspects of governance and delivery are delegated to the principal and his or her executive team. In good practice there will be a clear written schedule of Delegation to the Principal and others authorized by the governing body.

Likewise it is the governing body that enters into contractual arrangements with third parties, or authorizes such arrangements, particularly with its Funding Council, Research Council or others.

In greater detail the governing body of the institution shall create, or cause to be created, a strategic vision and consequent strategic planning processes. Clearly this vision will be influenced by stakeholder conditions, but will be owned by the institution, which has autonomy in determining its direction. It is for the governing body to ensure that such direction gains extensive third party support.

Beyond such strategy setting, the institution will create annual business plans, most of which will be in the public domain and will be fully disclosed to key stakeholders, such as its funding council. Subject to any imposed conditions as to use of allocated funds, the governing body can itself determine how to allocate capital, revenue or human resource.

All institutions are subject to course approval and monitoring by quality assurance agencies (state funded) across the component parts of the United Kingdom. Such monitoring is consistent across institutions, both by written submission, but also institutional visits, particularly through Enhancement-Led Institutional Reviews. In addition monitoring is undertaken by the funding councils as a pre-requisite of funding provision. In regard to this each funding council receives an annual ministerial letter of direction which is then used to direct policy by the boards of each funding council for the institutions for which they have responsibility.

Finally beyond internal examination of students, for degree and final examinations there will be an external examiner for individual courses, appointed by the institution through its academic board or senate. This represents an important aspect of ensuring objectivity in examination results and degree ratings.

Governing bodies vary in size, but on average a composition of 25 would not be untypical. Depending upon the age of the institution there will also be a senate or academic board, which may have a significant membership. In the last 25 years there has been a trend to the governance of institutions to move to smaller and more heavily engaged members of governing bodies. The reason for this is narrated earlier in this section as governing bodies have accepted greater collective and individual responsibilities. Typically a member of a governing body would be expected to commit up to 15 days per year to the institution and the chair up to 30 days.

Governing bodies will typically contain elected staff and student representatives, some ex-officio members usually drawn from the local community and others who are appointed. For those who are appointed, most governing bodies now advertise vacant positions having previously determined what skills are then required. It remains exceptional for remuneration to be offered to such appointees, although some chairs are now remunerated.

For further information about the UK higher education system see www.sfc.ac.uk; www.hefce.ac.uk.

Section Three: Recent Reforms That Have Taken Place Related to Governance

Whilst broadly governance structures have not to an external observer appeared to alter materially, there has in fact been significant change. When Gordon Brown was Chancellor of the Exchequer in 2002 he became exercised about the failure of the University of Oxford to admit a talented young woman from a disadvantaged background. She thereafter gained a scholarship to Harvard University. The Chancellor invited Richard Lambert, the retiring editor of the *Financial Times,* to lead a review of governance and business-university collaboration—see reference links at the end of this section.

- The Committee of University Chairs (CUC) in 2004 in response to the Lambert Report in updating guidance for governors created a Governance Code of Practice and General Principles of governance. This Code was and is voluntary, but has gained the widest recognition by institutions, Treasury, funding councils and other stakeholders.
- Whilst voluntary, all UK institutions make reference to the Code in their annual corporate governance statements. As with other codes in the United Kingdom, particularly for stock exchange purposes, it is for each institution to indicate if it has had regard to the Code and if not in detail, why not. The Code and the extensive guidance, now available to governors is accessed in the link at the end of this section.
- The importance of the Code was to make abundantly clear where responsibility lay with detailed descriptions in the supporting Guide material for governing bodies the principal and executive and other stakeholders.

The Code and CUC Guide for Governors was updated in February 2009 linked to further work under the title is also accessible below.

For further information about recent reforms see: www.hm-treasury.gov.uk/lambert; www.shef.ac.uk.

Section Four: Lessons for Other Countries

The United Kingdom has what is widely regarded as an autonomous sector. Lessons learned include the following:

- If there is to be real autonomy for individual institutions and the sector there needs to be clear and unambiguous accountability by governing bodies, both in legal and reputational terms. The Code referred to in the previous section emphasize such obligations.

- Greater accountability will be accepted, if embraced voluntarily by the sector rather than imposed by regulation. However, the UK experience from both the standpoint of the state (through the Treasury) and the sector was that it was the threat of greater state control and intervention in 2002, which united the sector to take action. This led to the state accepting the value in offering greater autonomy under "a right touch" regime of scrutiny. Conversely individual institutions responded positively to the acceptance of enhanced responsibility.

- In a time of economic challenge part of autonomy and accountability is an acceptance both by state and institutions that individual institutions may fail. They will not be rescued by greater state funding if they do so fail. In consequence there is greater collaboration occurring between and amongst institutions to gain greater efficiencies. There is, however, no discernable trend towards merger.

Autonomy and Accountability in the United States of America[18]

In the United States, the differing roles of the federal and state governments and the diversity of the higher education system, including public, private nonprofit, and for-profit institutions, strongly influence the nature of autonomy and accountability. The fifty state governments, not the federal government, have primary responsibility for education, yet the federal government plays significant but different role in higher education policy.[19]

The state role is carried out primarily through state colleges and universities or local colleges operating within the framework of state law. State and local institutions constitute 41 percent of the institutions and enroll 76 percent of the students in the United States. In order to operate, all institutions, public, private nonprofit or for-profit, must be chartered or licensed by a state. All, but three, small states have established statewide boards or agencies for planning, coordination and oversight of their higher education systems. The primary means of state financing of higher education is through subsidy of public colleges and universities. Nevertheless, most states provide significant funding directly to students who attend both public and private institutions, and a few states also provide direct subsidy of private institutions for specific purposes.[20]

The federal government carries out its role not through subsidy of institutions (except for institutions such as the major military academies) but through student grants and loans and through largely competitive funding for research and development. Federal policy generally makes no distinction between public and private institutions, provided the institutions meet the basic eligibility requirements.

Despite its limited role in providing direct institutional subsidy, the federal government also plays a prominent role in defining basic accountability requirements that affect institutional substantive and procedural autonomy. These requirements affect both public and private institutions. These include, among other points:

- Tax policies governing nonprofit institutions, investments and other dimensions of institutional finance
- Accounting standards
- Constitutional and other legal requirements regarding equal opportunity and affirmative action
- The requirements that an institution must be accredited by a federally-approved accrediting agency to be eligible for federal funding
- Federally mandated data collection requirements
- Federally mandated reporting requirements on issues like graduation rates, campus crime or potential terrorist threats
- Detailed accountability requirements linked to federal contracts and grants governing financial management as well as issues such as stem-cell research and intellectual property.

Consequently, even though well-known institutions such as Harvard, M.I.T., Yale, University of Pennsylvania, or Stanford are private, they face significant federal accountability requirements as do their counterparts in the public sector.

Historically, the states have accorded both public and private institutions a high degree of substantive autonomy. Even public institutions that are often subject to extensive procedural administrative, management and financial regulation have traditionally been granted significant substantive autonomy. Following the principles established by the Supreme Court's ruling in *Dartmouth College v. Woodward* in 1819, state governments have been reluctant to intrude in core issues of academic policy at either public or private institutions. Rather than govern public institutions directly, state governments rely upon boards of trustees or governors composed of citizens representing the public interest as the means to ensure public accountability.[21]

With only a few exceptions, state governments impose few accountability requirements on private institutions. For these institutions, the federal government, not the states, is the source of the most demanding accountability requirements. The most common state requirements are those that apply to all private corporations in terms of fiscal integrity, consumer protection, environmental impact and similar non-academic issues. The other common accountability requirements stem from private institutions' participation in state student financial aid or other grant programs. In an increasing number of states, private institutions are participating voluntarily on state data systems in order to ensure that their contributions to serving the state's population are recognized in state planning.[22]

The 50 states differ markedly in the extent to which they grant public universities procedural autonomy. The trend is for states to move universities from the status of state agencies with extensive state procedural controls, to "state-related" or in some cases "corporate" status.

In several states, the major "state" universities are technically private corporations chartered by the state to serve pubic purposes. Pennsylvania State University, the University of Pittsburg, and Temple Universities are examples of this legal status. Even within the same state, governments may accord different levels of autonomy to different sectors. For example, the University of California has greater procedural autonomy from state government than the California State University System.

U.S. State of Virginia[23]

Section One: Context, Size, and Shape of the Higher Education Sector

Virginia has 120 HEIs enrolling 457,863 students (338,960 on a full-time equivalent basis). Most students are enrolled in public institutions. The state has a large public community college (2-year) system enrolling 160,576 students. Public universities enroll 197,247 students.

Table 4.6. Higher Education Sector in Virginia, USA

	Total	Private, for profit		Private, nonprofit		Public	
		2-year	4-year	2-year	4-year	2-year	4-year
Number of institutions	120	21	20	4	36	24	15
Full-time equivalent enrollment	338,960	8,463	17,818	754	58,129	87,407	166,389
Headcount enrollment	457,863	8,917	20,916	934	69,273	160,576	197,247
Number of full-time faculty	14,693	198	533	N/A	3,536	2,139	8,287

Source: National Center for Education Statistics, IPEDS, 2007.
Notes: "4-year" institution references to colleges and universities that grant the baccalaureate degree and above.

Fourteen (14) institutions grant professional engineering degrees (2 for-profit private institutions, 3 non-for-profit private institutions, and 9 public institutions). Thirty-four institutions grant technology degrees of which 24 are two-year community colleges.

In 2007, Virginia institutions granted 2,089 undergraduate (baccalaureate) degrees in various professional engineering fields, 949 master's degrees in engineering, and 249 doctoral degrees. At the level of engineering technology, most degrees granted were at the certificate or associate-degree level (588) and the remainder (224) at the baccalaureate level.

None of the institutions in Virginia has a mission focused only on engineering and technology. Virginia Polytechnic Institute and State University (Virginia Tech) grants the largest number of engineering degrees, followed by University of Virginia and George Mason University. Virginia Tech grants 21 percent of its degrees in engineering fields, the highest concentration of engineering of any public university in Virginia.

Although the state's public universities are state owned and controlled, they receive on average only 27 percent of their revenue from state appropriations, while 29 percent of their revenue comes from student tuition and fees, 17 percent from endowment earnings, and the remainder from a variety of other public and private sources.

Virginia's private institutions are funded primarily from student tuition and fees. Private nonprofit institutions also receive funding from endowment earnings, private giving, and restricted-purpose federal and state grants and contracts.

Section Two: Specific Governance Arrangements

According to the Constitution of Virginia,[24] the Commonwealth has three distinct and separate branches of government: the legislature, the executive, and judiciary. The Governor is elected for a term of four years and can serve only one term, a provision that has the effect of limiting the extent to which any single governor can major significant changes in state policy.

Public higher education in Virginia has a decentralized governing structure within the framework of state planning and coordination. Each of the 15 public universities has a governing board, called a "Board of Visitors," whose members are appointed by the Governor and confirmed by the State Senate. The public community colleges are governed by a single State Board for Community Colleges and each college has a local board with advisory powers.

The formal responsibilities of Boards of Visitors[25] are to:

- Provide oversight and leadership at their respective institutions
- Set broad policy goals and priorities for their institutions
- Select a President to manage the day-to-day operations
- Evaluate the President to ensure compliance with statutory mandates and board goals, priorities, and directives
- Establish rules and regulations for the admission of students and graduation requirements, conduct of students, employment of professors, teachers, instructors, and all other employees and provide for their dismissal for failure to abide by such rules and regulations
- Review and approve budget requests to the Governor and General Assembly for state appropriations
- Ensure academic integrity at the institution, including, reviewing the curriculum and faculty productivity
- Set tuition and fee charges
- Lease, sell, or convey any and all real estate with the approval of the Governor
- Provide oversight of institutionally affiliated foundations
- Ensure institution is accountable for the effective and efficient use of Virginia taxpayer dollars provided to it.

The State Council of Higher Education for Virginia (SCHEV) has statutory responsibility for state-wide planning and coordination, program approval for public universities and community colleges, and development of all budget guidelines and formulas, reviewing institutional budgets and making recommendations to the Governor and General Assembly in areas of capital and operating budget planning, enrollment projections, institutional technology needs, and student financial aid. The Council consists of 11 members appointed by the governor with confirmation by the State Senate.

Despite the appearance of a decentralized governance structure in which the institutional Boards of Visitors have broad authority and responsibility, the reality is that Virginia historically has had a higher level of financial and administrative oversight than many of the public higher education systems in the United States.

Except as modified by the 2005 Restructuring Act, public institutions are subject to the same oversight as any other state agency by the State Attorney General and more than ten state departments under the jurisdiction of the Governor's Cabinet Secretaries of Education, Administration, Finance and Technology.

The status of public HEIs as "state agencies" has meant that financial operations have been highly interwoven with the rest of state government. Over the years, the authority to establish tuition and fees and to management revenue from these and other "non-state" sources has been one of the most contentious issues. It was this issue, among others, that became the focus of debate leading to the 2005 Restructuring Act.[26]

Section Three: Recent Reforms[27]

The 2005 Restructuring Act was the culmination of more than a decade of debate about decentralization and increasing autonomy for public institutions in Virginia. The final legislation represented the convergence of two initiatives.

The Restructuring Act establishes three levels of autonomy, each reflecting different levels of capacity and readiness of institutions to assume responsibility for higher levels of autonomy:

- **Level I:** All public colleges are eligible for increased operational autonomy in areas including procurement, leases, personnel, and capital outlay.
- **Level II:** Institutions may seek additional operational autonomy through a memorandum of understanding (MOU) with the appropriate cabinet secretary in the areas of information technology and/or human resources and personnel.
- **Level III:** Institutions that can demonstrate advanced financial and administrative strength may seek additional, more comprehensive autonomy through a management agreement, which outlines board-approved policies in the following areas: 1) capital outlay; 2) leases; 3) information technology; 4) procurement; 5) human resources; and 6) finance and accounting.[28]

To eligible for Level I autonomy, each institution's Board of Visitors must act to commit to meet specific performance requirements. Then each institution's performance must be certified annually by the State Council of Higher Education for Virginia. The performance requirements, based on the Governor's original priorities, include:

- Ensure access to higher education, including meeting enrollment demand
- Ensure affordability to Virginia students, regardless of income
- Provide a broad range of academic programs
- Maintain high academic standards
- Improve student retention and progress toward timely graduation
- Develop uniform articulation agreements with community colleges
- Stimulate economic development, and for those seeking further autonomy, assume additional responsibility for economic development in distressed areas
- Where appropriate, increase externally funded research and improve technology transfer
- Work actively with public education (kindergarten through grade 12) to improve student achievement
- Prepare a six-year financial plan
- Meet financial and administrative management standards
- Ensure campus safety and security.[29] As of the latest annual certification process, all public universities have been certified as meeting the performance requirements for Level I, although several institutions have been required to take action to improve performance in specific areas.[30]

The Restructuring Act provides financial incentives for institutions achieving Level I autonomy, including interest earnings on funds that the institutions have deposited into the state treasury and automatic re-appropriation of unexpended year-end balances.[31]

Institutions seeking Level III autonomy must enter into management agreements with the Commonwealth and meet certain high levels of performance in terms of financial integrity and performance in pilot projects in specific areas of increased autonomy. Three universities have entered into such agreements. The Restructuring Act presumably granted public institutions at Level III with addition flexibility regarding tuition policy.[32]

Section Four: Lessons for Other Countries

The most significant issues related to institutional autonomy often concern general government laws and policies that affect all state entities, not only public colleges and universities. These include, among others (1) finance policies governing the allocate of public funding, the disposition and investment of non-state revenue; and (2) human resource policies: pay scales, civil service protections, health, and retirement programs

The government must make explicit its public priorities as a foundation for public accountability.

- Accountability must be for performance related to both public priorities as well as key administrative and financial indicators
- Initiatives to increase autonomy must take into consideration differences among institutions in capacity to assume the additional responsibilities that are entailed by autonomy
- Reform should be shaped in a manner that will have benefits in the long run for the whole higher education sector, not just a few universities
- The effectiveness of institutional governing boards (called Boards of Visitors in Virginia) is fundamental to the success of decentralized governance and public accountability
- The number and complexity of institutional performance standards can overwhelm and defeat the purposes of the accountability process
- The developing special agreements (management agreements, memorandums of understanding, contracts) with each institution to provide exceptions to a multitude of state laws and regulations can become a bureaucratic nightmare.

Notes

[1] By Arun Nigavekar, Raja Ramanna Fellow, Department of Atomic Energy, Senior Advisor, Science and Technology Park, University of Pune, and former Chairman of the Indian University Grants Commission.

[2] All India Council of Technical Education (AICTE), Medical Council of India (MCI), Indian Council for Agricultural Research (ICAR), National Council for Teacher Education (NCTE) , Dental Council of India (DCI) , Pharmacy Council of India (PCI) , Indian Nursing Council (INC) , Bar Council of India (BCI) , Central Council of Homeopathy (CCH) , Central Council for Indian Medicine (CCIM) , Council of Architecture , Distance Education Council , Rehabilitation Council , National Council for Rural Institutes , State Councils of Higher Education

[3] By Rong Wang, Professor at the China Institute for Educational Finance Research, Peking University.

[4] Data source for quoted statistics figures: Educational Statistics Yearbook of China 2007. Exceptions are noted in the text.

[5] Classification of HEIs: comprehensive university, HEIs of natural sciences and technology, HEIs of agriculture, HEIs of forestry, HEIs of medicine and pharmacy, HEIs of teacher training, HEIs of language and literature, HEIs of finance and economics, HEIs of political science and law, HEIs of physical culture, HEIs of art, and HEIs of ethnic nationality. It should be noted that of all the 1015 tertiary vocational and technical colleges, only 449 are classified as HEIs of natural sciences and technology.

[6] Classification of field of study: philosophy, economics, law, education, literature, history, science, engineering, agriculture, medicine, administration.

[7] By Tsutomu Kimura, President of the National Institute of Academic Degrees and University Evaluation in Japan and former President of Tokyo Institute of Technology.

[8] For a more detailed description and breakdown of Japanese higher education see: http://www.mext.go.jp/english/koutou/index.htm, and the OECD published report 2008: http://www.oecd.org/dataoecd/44/12/42280329.pdf.

[9] By Aims McGuinness, Senior Associate of the National Center for Higher Education Management Systems (NCHEMS) in the United States and former chair of the Board of Trustees of the State Colleges in Colorado.

[10] The founder of national universities is the national government. The founders of public universities are autonomous local governments.

[11] Private universities are subject to specific laws, including the Private School Act. Private universities must be founded by educational corporations. Educational corporations may freely decide on issues regarding the organization and operation of the board of directors and the appointment of executives as long as the issue is not mentioned in the private school act. Private universities are heavily relying on tuition. The transfer of educational finances to other areas is restricted by separating school finances from corporate financing. In order to secure transparency in school finances, the budget and settlement of accounts of private institutions are opened on the website for the university. In addition, in order to protect the assets of educational corporations, basic requirements as seen in related laws on the disposal of university assets such as receiving the approval of the respective authority in selling, donating, and warranting assets of the educational corporation must be followed.

[12] Byun, Kiyong (2008), p. 6.

[13] Byun, Kiyong, (2008), p. 7.

[14] Government of Korea, Ministry of Education, Science and Technology, "Major Policies to Enhance the Competitive Strength of Korean Higher Education," February 2009. http://english.mest.go.kr/main.jsp?idx=0301020101&brd_no=52&cp=1&pageSize=10&srchSel=&srchVal=&brd_mainno=878&mode=v.

[15] This summary draws on Byun (2008).

[16] By Aims McGuinness, Senior Associate of the National Center for Higher Education Management Systems (NCHEMS) in the United States, and former chair of the Board of Trustees of the State Colleges in Colorado.

[17] By Andrew Cubie, Chair of the Court of Napier University, The Scottish Credit and Qualification Framework, and former Chair of the University Chairs of the UK; and Jannette Cheong, Advisor on International Collaboration Initiatives and former Head of International Collaboration and Development, Higher Education Funding Council for England.

[18] By Aims McGuinness, Senior Associate of the National Center for Higher Education Management Systems (NCHEMS) in the United States, and former chair of the Board of Trustees of the State Colleges in Colorado.

[19] Zumeta, W. (2004) "Accountability and the Private Sector: State and Federal Perspectives," *Achieving Accountability in Higher Education: Balancing Public, Academic and Market Demands*, Burke, J., and Associates, eds., San Francisco: Jossey-Bass, pp. 25-54.

[20] McGuinness, A. (2005). "The States and Higher Education," *American Higher Education in the Twenty-First Century*. Altbach, P., Berdahl, R., and Gumport, P., eds., Baltimore: Johns Hopkins University Press, pp. 198-225.

[21] Zumeta, W. (2004), p. 28.

[22] Zumeta, W. (2004). P. 26.

[23] By Aims McGuinness, Senior Associate of the National Center for Higher Education Management Systems (NCHEMS) in the United States, and former chair of the Board of Trustees of the State Colleges in Colorado.

[24] Constitution of the Commonwealth of Virginia, July 1971 with amendments through 2007, Articles I, section 5.

[25] As summarized on SCHEV website.

[26] Couturier, Lara K. (2006). "Checks and Balances at Work: The Restructuring of Virginia's Public Higher Education System." San Jose: National Center for Public Policy and Higher Education, June 2006. See the following link for copy of full report: http://www.highereducation.org/reports/checks_balances/

[27] This section draws extensively on an excellent case study of the Restructuring Act written by Lara K. Couturier. See the following link for copy of full report: http://www.highereducation.org/reports/checks_balances/.

[28] Couturier, p. 27.

[29] Couturier, pp. 20-21

[30] See State Council of Higher Education website for 2009 certification actions: http://research.schev.edu/ips/review/certification_action_2009.asp.

[31] Couturier, p. 27.

[32] See summary of 2009 Tuition and Fees presented to House Appropriations Committee by the State Council of Higher Education: http://www.schev.edu/council/presentations/HAC%20presentation%20(6-16-09).pdf.

Appendixes

Appendix A. List of Participants

NAME	TEAM	TITLE
Ms Rashmi Chowdhary	MHRD	Director
Ambadas U Digraskar	NPIU	Central Project Advisor
Rita Goyal	NPIU	Consultant
S Ramachandran	NPIU	Consultant
Sachin Gupta	NPIU	Consultant
Suresh Chanda	Andhra Pradesh	Principal Secretary Higher Education
K C Reddy	Andhra Pradesh	Chairman, State Council for Higher Education
L Premachandra Reddy	Andhra Pradesh	Commissioner of Technical Education
A V Srikanth	Andhra Pradesh	TEQIP Coordinator, SPFU, Deputy Director of Technical Education
Ramachandram	Andhra Pradesh	TEQIP Coordinator, OUCE, Hyderabad
P S N Raju	Andhra Pradesh	Principal, Andhra University College of Engineering Vishakapatnam
N V Ramana Rao	Andhra Pradesh	Principal, JNTU College of Engineering, Hyderabad
P Narsimha Reddy	Andhra Pradesh	Director, Sreenidhi Institute of Science, and Technology, Hyderabad
M P Gupta	Haryana	Director-cum-SPFU Head, Technical Education
R K Miglani	Haryana	Deputy Secretary, SPFU Haryana
H S Chaha	Haryana	Vice Chancellor, Deenbandhu Chhotu Ram University of S&T
Ashok Arora	Haryana	Director, YMCA Institute of Engineering, Faridabad
C.P.Kaushik	Haryana	TEQIP Coordinator, Guru Jambheshwar University of S&T
B R Marwah	Haryana	Executive Director, N.C. College of Engineering, Israna, Panipat
V R Singh	Haryana	Director, PDM Educational Institutions, Sarai Aurangabad
A S Srikanth	Karnataka	State Secretary
H U Talawar	Karnataka	Director of Technical Education
Aravind Kulkarni	Karnataka	Project Officer, SPFU
M Raghunath	Karnataka	Project Officer, SPFU
B Sangameshwar	Karnataka	Principal, SJCE, Mysore
Dr Rajanikanth	Karnataka	Principal, MSRIT, Bangalore
GP Prabhu Kumar	Karnataka	Principal, Acharya Institute of Tech, Bangalore
Raja Rao	Karnataka	Principal, R.V. College of Engineering, Bangalore.

NAME	TEAM	TITLE
J S Sahariya	Maharashtra	Principal Secretary, Higher, and Technical Education Dept.,
S K Mahajan	Maharashtra	Director, Technical Education
Vinod Mohitkar	Maharashtra	Deputy Director of Technical Education
Abhay Wagh	Maharashtra	Dy. Director, Technical Education
B B Ahuja	Maharashtra	Dy. Director, COE, Pune
W Z Gandhare	Maharashtra	Principal, GCOE, Aurangabad
Sharad Mhaiskar	Maharashtra	Principal, SPCE, Andheri, Mumbai
A S Pant	Maharashtra	Principal, GCOE, Karad
Manotosh Biswas	West Bengal	Special Secretary, Higher Education Department
Sajal Dasgupta	West Bengal	Director of Technical Education, Head, SPFU
Sabyasachi Sengupta	West Bengal	V.C., West Bengal University of Technology
Manoj Mitra	West Bengal	Dean of Faculty of Engineering, and Technology, Jadavpur University
Satyajit Chakraborty	West Bengal	Director, Institute of Engineering, and Management
Buddhadeb Chattopadhyay	West Bengal	Principal, Government College of Engineering and Leather Technology
B B Paira	West Bengal	Director, Heritage Institute of Technology
Rajdeep Sahrawat	NASSCOM	Vice President
Avneet Bajaj	NASSCOM	Senior Manager, Education Initiative
Sandhya Chintala	NASSCOM	Director, Education Initiatives
Bidhan Kankate	NASSCOM	Regional Director, Andhra Pradesh
Shruti Verma	NASSCOM	Senior Associate, Initiatives, and *Forums*
P Arjun	NASSCOM	Senior Associate, Membership, and Events
Sudhanva	NASSCOM	Manager, Business Development
Jannette Cheong	World Bank	Consultant, international expert team
Andrew Cubie	World Bank	Consultant, international expert team
Aims McGuinness	World Bank	Consultant, international expert team
Arun Nigavekar	World Bank	Consultant, international expert team
Tom Kimura	World Bank	Consultant, international expert team
Andreas Blom	World Bank	SASHD, Project Leader
Meera Chatterjee	World Bank	SASDI, Senior Social Development Specialist
Hiroshi Saeki	World Bank	SASHD, Operations Analyst
Kurt Larsen	World Bank	WBIHD, Education Specialist
Anne Kroijer	World Bank	WBIHD, Consultant
Vijay Thadani	Evening speaker	CEO, NIIT; Chairman of CII National Committee on Education
S P K Naidu	Evening speaker	Special Chief Secretary to Government of Andhra Pradesh
D N Reddy	Evening speaker	Vice Chancellor, JNTU, Andhra Pradesh

Appendix B. Some Observations and Lessons for Future Learning Fora

Inputs

The overall size and composition of the *Forum* was considered critical. Too many would inhibit participation and restrict discussion. Too few would not be cost effective and would impact on the overall value to the participants. Composition of the state representatives was chosen by the states themselves and the number decided by the *Forum* team to ensure a good balance of policy and practice leaders.

Other key stakeholder groups were represented, but these were fewer in number. This did not lessen the either the importance nor the impact of their contribution – which was both essential and excellent, but allowed for more state and institutional representatives to attend and participate as the target audience of policymakers and practitioners responsible for leading and implementing change in the participating states and institutions. It is clear that these leaders will need to work in partnership with industry and other stakeholders. It was also clear that this is welcomed by industry and the state leaders and will be taken forward in future in a number of ways, some of which will be led by industry bodies such as NASSCOM.

The *Learning Forum* required a significant amount of content preparation by the core *Forum* team and participants. A half-day planning meeting was held in the National Institute of Technology, Warangal in January 2009 and a *planning document* was produced setting out overall objectives, background, methodology, success criteria, stakeholder analysis and other necessary background information, including common priorities and challenges identified by the five states in Warangal.[1]

Forum preparation, materials, and presentations were kept to concise formats a) to reduce the amount of work required for any one person/state, and b) to help focus time and attention to key matters. As part of the preparation each state nominated a senior colleague who participated in audio conferences with core *Forum* team members, and was responsible for all state communications, facilitation and preparation work. Even so some states responded later than others for various reasons and this resulted in less time available for participants to read documentation in advance, as well as putting pressure on those administering the *Forum*.

Getting the timing right was a challenge—elections, festival holidays and availability of participants and contributors. The *Forum* was postponed once because it was not possible to coordinate these various factors. Despite these initial setbacks it should be noted that the high level of commitment from senior officials was exemplary. Their leadership was key to the excellent outputs and outcomes of the *Forum*, and has set a high standard for others to follow at future *Fora*.

The following papers were prepared in advance of the *Learning Forum* to provide an appropriate basis and comparative context for discussions:

- A national case study of India
- Six international case studies
- Five state case studies
- 20 institutional case studies, 17 from participating states, and three international institutional case studies
- Four generic papers relating to the principles and challenges of governance and international trends.

Inputs from Key Note Speakers

The *Learning Forum* heard from other stakeholders. Although few in number, their messages were clear and made a substantial impact on *Forum* participants. Mr. S.P.K. Naidu I.A.S, Special Chief Secretary, Andhra Pradesh emphasized the need for change in the levels of investment and funding for higher education, and in tackling the three major problems of quality, access and employability.

Professor K. C. Reddy, Chairman of the Andra Pradesh State Council Higher Education participated as a member in the panel during the session on "Why is governance Important" and focused on the importance of good governance for the society, students, and parents, government and institution. Professor Reddy emphasized three critical aspects of Higher Education expansion: equity, quality and relevance.

There were three other key inputs from industry-related stakeholders. Mr Rajdeep Sahrawat, Vice-President of NASSCOM joined the panel who answered questions on Why good governance was important to stakeholders and responded to participants questions about the urgent needs of industry for suitably qualified and experienced graduates in contributing to India's rapidly expanding knowledge economy.

Dr Sandhya Chintala, Director, Education Initiatives, NASSCOM, joined the 'Question Time' panel. Panel members were interrogated on questions related to quality assurance and review strategies needed to monitor policy and practice. Dr Chintala also made a short, but clear presentation on the NAC-Tech initiative towards the end of the *Learning Forum* as an example of industry taking the initiative on the important issues of the assessment of student outcomes and competences with reference to capacity building and employability, essential in an internationally competitive market.

Finally, Mr Vijay Thadani made a 'call to arms' speech in the evening of Day Two. He raised five major issues:

- India's low gross enrollment ratio, which he said will not reach the world average even by the end of 13th five-year plan at the current rate of investment/development. He declared that India has both some of the best and worst educational outcomes.
- The challenges of improving partnership working between industry, society, education policy makers, education practitioners and 'skill developers'. At the moment, he commented, these are like 'five Pacific Islands with only an occasional ferry service.
- The need for a common understanding of 'quality' across the country because Quality is fundamental.
- The importance of thinking 'big' in order to achieve big results.
- And finally, that India was not alone. The whole world is grappling with the transition of higher education—India can be a beacon.

The World Bank set up a pilot website for the *Learning Forum* prior to the start of the project to ensure that all materials produced would be available as soon as possible after the conclusion of the *Forum,* with the goal that this would be migrated to the TEQIP website in due course. It will be the responsibility of TEQIP-II to decide how this material and the site will be managed in future in support of their work. There is a question about how interactive the site could be to support a greater flow of communication, ideas and sharing of experience between *Learning Forum* participants and others. However, such development of the site will clearly depend on 'demand for such services' and available technical and other resources.

Funding for the *Learning Forum* was organized by the World Bank in discussion with National and state governments. During the planning stage the British Council also provided some funds to support the attendance of two of the independent consultants at the planning meeting in Warangal. While the resounding feedback at the end of the *Forum* was positive, the real evaluation and benefit of such activities can only be made when seen against the actions taken at the state and institutional level.

Process

The *Forum* aimed to build a **bridge between policy and practice**. The format of the three, over four, day residential *Forum,* included principally:

■ First half of the *Forum* focused at state level, the second at the institutional level, finishing with conclusions related to both states and institutions

■ A mix of focused plenary and small group work facilitated debate and discussion

■ Plenary sessions using short presentations, and panels who responded to focused questioning from participants

■ Invited speakers principally: Mr. S.P.K. Naidu I.A.S, Special Chief Secretary, Andhra Pradesh, and Mr. Vijay Thadani, CEO, NIIT and Prof D N Reddy, Vice Chancellor, JNTU, Andhra Pradesh.

The number of days was allowed so that sufficient time could be spent with both policymakers and institutional leaders. However, given the amount of shared input achieved during the pilot it is clear that it could be possible to reduce the overall length of the *Forum*, at least by one day, for future such events. And, indeed, consider a variety of lengths of fora—for example, some states are planning shorter one-day follow-up fora for the future.

The methodology was based initially on the notion of a *Learning Journey*[2] to set a simple progressive framework for understanding developments and challenges for India (and also, for comparative benchmarking purposes, international references were included). Conceptually, this seemed to work well for participants, as a vehicle for learning and to help focus aspects of the discussion on the *current situation (Where we are now), direction and aspirations (Where are we going), implementation and actions (How will we get there?), and most importantly evaluating actions taken (both policy and practice) (How will we know if we have been successful).*

Forum participants debated extensively priorities for action and implementation plans. *Who, does what, with whom, to what effect?* State officials and institutional leaders and industry participants used a variety of formats and opportunities to express their views, expectations and requirements. To this extent, the *Learning Journey* conceptual framework was a helpful vehicle. But, as can be seen by the outcomes, the multi-layered and interlinked challenges cannot be underestimated. It will require a lot of partnership working, respecting the needs of the various stakeholders and finding meaningful and authoritative channels to ensure that proper consultation is undertaken regarding the various governance issues being addressed.

Another key aspect of the *Learning Forum* was the use of international case studies. It was considered important for those leading developments in India to set these against what is happening internationally, and to appreciate lessons learned elsewhere—both inside and outside India.

Based on the experience and feedback gained from the pilot *Learning Forum* in Hyderabad, and at the planning meeting at NIT Warangal, participants were asked, and willingly accepted, to share their experience and learning with other states and centrally funded institutions across India.

Participants' attendance at the *Learning Forum* was formally recognized by the World Bank and NASSCOM.

Additional General Comments Regarding Outputs and Outcomes

When the participants began this *Learning Journey* in NIT Warangal in January 2009 they identified the following common priorities and challenges from the five participating states:

- How individual institutions can meet the demands of stakeholders within a more autonomous and accountable system
- How individual states and institutions can develop their capacity to deliver the wider needs of communities and tackle important equity issues
- How institutions can address internal capacity needs across a range of academic, administrative and management areas
- How confusion of roles can be avoided, and the need for greater clarity between state and institutional governance responsibilities
- How the *Forum* could support benchmarking and the sharing of information between and beyond states, including key performance indicators
- How the involvement of industry could be strengthened
- How individual states might feel it was important to look at failures, and to try to understand why these had occurred. They indicated that although they had made much progress in regard to governance there was a sense of urgency about their need to improve further. It was suggested that there were *'no soft options'* if states were to implement changes, strengthen accountability and make the sector more workable and feasible in the Indian context
- How there was a need to develop a more sustainable financial model—for institutions, both public and private
- How there was a need for a new look at delivering education to the rural areas. There was also the role that technology could play given the shortage of teachers and the need to deliver education, and the expansion of student numbers, in a more cost effective way.

The *Learning Forum* was able to explore in some depth many of these areas and share ideas about some of the underlying factors as they relate to governance. It was not for the *Learning Forum* to say which solutions would be appropriate for any state. There could be a number of solutions to a single problem. Nevertheless, important governance issues identified at the *Forum* were clearly articulated and agreed through discussion both between states and separately.

Critically, the *Learning Forum* provided a useful environment for senior policy makers and institutional leaders to agree nine key governance issues, using this as a tool for discussion to identify which of the issues related to institutions, state governments and central government. While many of these will involve education policy makers at the state and from central government working in partnership with institutions and other stakeholders, there remain actions that individual states and institutions can take without delay.

Such cross-state consensus is a valuable step forward in supporting national higher education developments and the national need for change management in higher education. By the end of the *Learning Forum* a number of participants articulated a keenness to take 'bold steps' and move outside of their 'comfort zone.'

All the participants of the *Learning Forum* have responsibilities for making effective changes either in terms of policy and/or practice. It is clear from the *Forum* that they are prepared to lead on this, but it is also clear some may feel dependent (and in some areas are not clear when they should not be dependent) on the leadership of others. Establishing the most effective way of making clear who will take the lead 'The Institution', 'The state', or a 'national body' and developing effective partnerships between these and other parties, including industry, will be critical to a number of key issues if this is not to be a barrier to the reforms envisaged.

The participants chose the verb 'to Learn' not only because it is most appropriate to the work that is central to participants' responsibilities that is, 'education', but also because it is central to managing change. As Aristotle said 'What we have to learn to do, we learn by doing.'

The *Learning Forum* appears to be timely. Industry leaders and politicians are making a 'call to arms'—but as participants identified, some of these challenges are short term and others are long term. But will they be long term because the process warrants a proper development over time, or just because implementation is not well thought through and fundamental needs not understood, or met?

Naturally, this crucial issue of timing and division of responsibility will be well considered as part of the planning and implementation for the next leg of these *Learning Journeys*. There will be a need for institutions, states, and central government to be clear about their targets, and to define what is meant by 'short, medium and long term.'

Hopefully, following the *Forum*, state and institutional leaders will be clearer about their roles and responsibilities as far as governance is concerned, and will be confident in their discussions with other stakeholders on the *Journey* that lies ahead.

As a concept, responsibility is not unlike power. Most people deny they have it—even those that are powerful—especially when difficult decisions need to be made. In reality, most people have a certain amount power and responsibility. Defining responsibilities and relationships sets appropriate boundaries and lies at the heart of 'good governance' and is one of the critical reasons why this cannot be an option.

Appendix C. Key Governance Issues Proforma

Key Governance Issues Proforma	For HEIs	For states	For the 'center' (national bodies)	Short term	Medium to long term
1. Conceptualize legal foundation for a **new model of an autonomous institution** to serve a public purpose. The model should be the same for institutions funded in part by the government as well as those receiving no government subsidy Transition all current government-funded, government-aided and private non-aided institutions to this model					
2. **Common legal framework for governance**, consistent with the new model of an autonomous institution, which provides:					
• **Clear statement of responsibilities and relationships** for the BOG, including composition of boards of governors, selection/nomination of members, powers and functions, and inculcation and assessment of accountability **(using national, UGC, guidelines)**					
• **Professional qualifications, experience, responsibilities and appointment** of the a) Vice Chancellor/Director, b) the senior institutional officials, c) Terms and conditions of service (minimum standards set by state) (implemented by HEI)					
• **Internal governing structure of the institution**, including the principal academic and administrative bodies within the institution					
3. **Strategic planning at institutional and state levels** to ensure: • Alignment with national and state priorities for India's global competitiveness in the knowledge economy:					
– Size, shape and relationship					
– Access and Equity					
– Affordability **(Needs Center support)**					
– Quality					
– Research Competitiveness					
– Inclusiveness (gender, ethnicity, etc.)					
• Responsiveness to the need of industry and India's future economy (credit transfer)					
4. Common quality assurance policies and standards (internationally benchmarked for example, internationally accepted parameters) and the needs of industry, including: • Common framework for qualifications, including the knowledge and skills required for employment and standards					
• Curriculum frameworks/subject benchmarks to guide curriculum development **(state/central government to specify minimum credits)**					
• Student assessment, and continuous quality improvement within institutions					
• Assessment and certification of skills and competencies obtained through industry-based training and experience for partial credit toward degrees					

Key Governance Issues Proforma	For HEIs	For states	For the 'center' (national bodies)	Short term	Medium to long term
• Quality assurance and accountability based on outcomes (at various levels) (institution +state)					
• Policies and mechanisms for student mobility (including credit transfer) within and between institutions and states, and outside India					
• Framework for faculty appraisal /faculty development scheme including training, need analysis and funding					
5. Policies and formal mechanisms for private industry/academic collaboration, including, but not limited to: • Industry investment in higher education (in kind, and funding) • Involving Industry in framing curriculum, skill development and evaluation of graduates.					
• Experts from private industry serving as faculty and researchers at institutions and faculty serving in industry					
• Industry providing training for students and awarding of credit for industry-based training					
6. Professional development for faculty, institutional leaders and boards of governors to increase their capacity to assume increased responsibilities in autonomous institutions (quality assurance, curriculum development, etc.)					
7. Optimum utilization of resources, including, but not limited to • Sharing of faculty and other resources (laboratories, libraries) among institutions					
• Use of technology for effective delivery of courses					
8. Technical assistance and mentoring ("hand-holding") for institutions making the transition to autonomous status.					
9. Policy to tackle faculty shortage					

Source: Author.

Notes

[1] See reference and outcomes in the **Planning Document** on the *Forum* website

[2] See *Forum* website for more information on the *Learning Journey* and *Forum* methodology

Eco-Audit

Environmental Benefits Statement

The World Bank is committed to preserving Endangered Forests and natural resources. We print World Bank Working Papers and Country Studies on postconsumer recycled paper, processed chlorine free. The World Bank has formally agreed to follow the recommended standards for paper usage set by Green Press Initiative—a nonprofit program supporting publishers in using fiber that is not sourced from Endangered Forests. For more information, visit www.greenpressinitiative.org.

In 2008, the printing of these books on recycled paper saved the following:

Trees*	Solid Waste	Water	Net Greenhouse Gases	Total Energy
289	8,011	131,944	27,396	92 mil.
*40 feet in height and 6–8 inches in diameter	Pounds	Gallons	Pounds CO_2 Equivalent	BTUs

green press
INITIATIVE